134945 FEB 09 FEB 12

D0947134

DATE DUE

HISTORY OF THE WORLD

Civilizations of the Americas

134945

RAINTREE PUBLISHERS
Milwaukee

This book has been reviewed for accuracy by
William Douglas Burgess, Jr., Dept. of History,
East Tennessee State University, Johnson City, Tennessee.

History of the World by Editoriale Jaca Book s.p.a., Milano. Copyright © 1987
by Editoriale Jaca Book.

English translation copyright © 1989 Raintree Publishers Limited Partnership.
Published in the United States by Raintree Publishers.

Translated by Hess-Inglin Translation Service.

All rights reserved. No part of this book may be reproduced or utilized in any
form or by any means, electronic or mechanical, including photocopying,
recording, or by any information storage and retrieval system, without permission
in writing from the Publisher. Inquiries should be addressed to Raintree
Publishers, 310 West Wisconsin Avenue, Milwaukee, Wisconsin 53203.

2 3 4 5 6 7 8 9   93 92 91 90

Library of Congress Number: 88-26416

Printed and bound in the United States of America.

Library of Congress Cataloging-in-Publication Data

Preistoria e civiltà delle Americhe. English.
  Civilization of the Americas.

  (History of the World)
  Translation of: Preistoria e civiltà delle Americhe.
  Includes index.
  Summary: Describes the early civilizations of North, Central, and South
America through the time of Columbus.
  1. Indians—Antiquities—Juvenile literature. 2. America—Antiquities—
Juvenile literature. [1. Indians—Antiquities. 2. America—Antiquities.]
  I. Raintree Publishers. II. Title. III. Series.
E61.P7513 1988   970.01   88-26416
ISBN 0-8172-3306-7

Cover illustration by Francis Balistreri.

TABLE OF CONTENTS

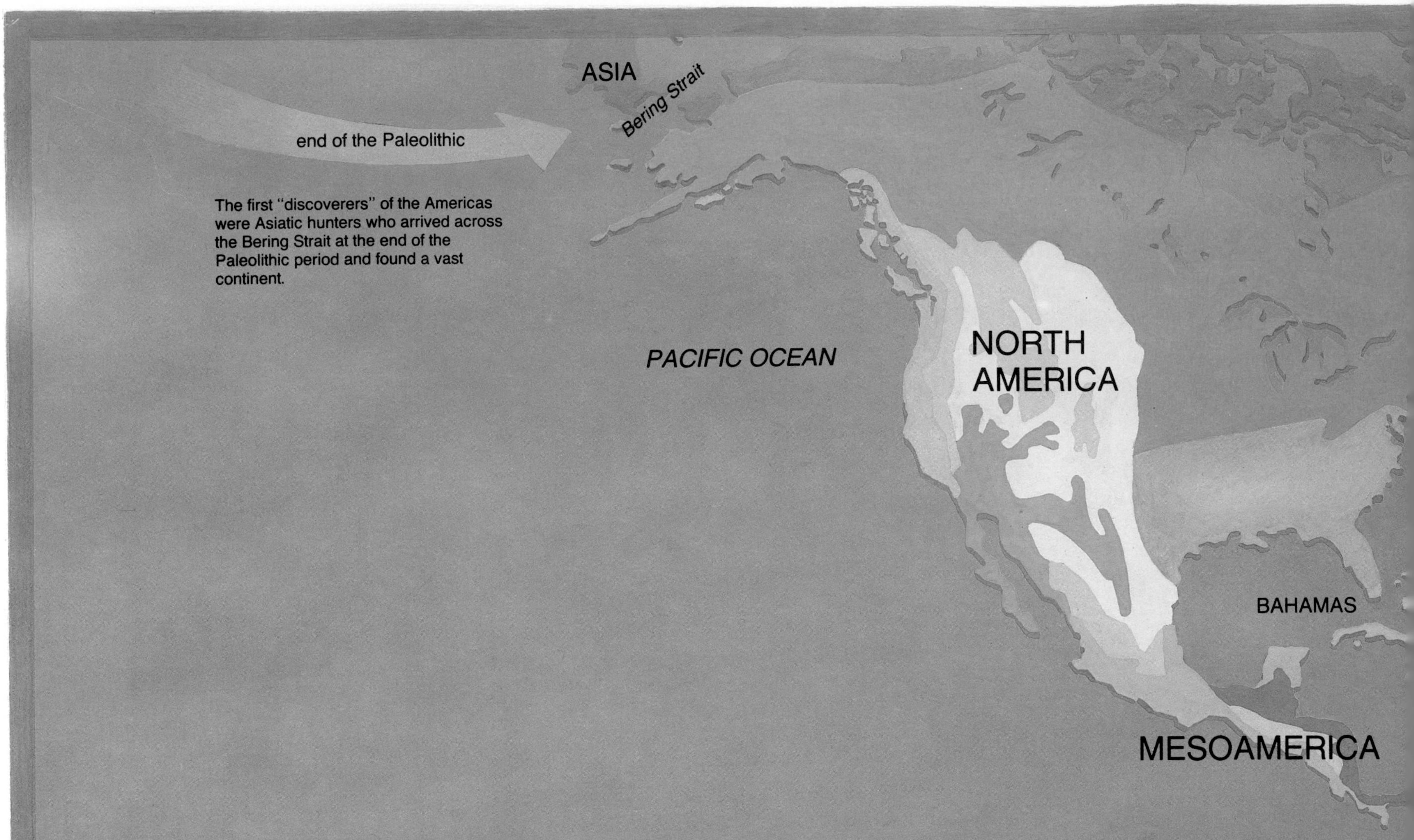

ASIA

Bering Strait

end of the Paleolithic

The first "discoverers" of the Americas were Asiatic hunters who arrived across the Bering Strait at the end of the Paleolithic period and found a vast continent.

PACIFIC OCEAN

NORTH AMERICA

BAHAMAS

MESOAMERICA

THE PHYSICAL AMERICAS

The New World landmass measures 9,000 miles (14,500 kilometers) from the Arctic to Cape Horn, both continents reaching 3,000 miles (4,800 km) across at their widest points. This immense territory covers one-quarter of the world's habitable surface.

The most impressive feature in North America is the Rocky Mountains, which run the length of the continent like a gigantic backbone. The Appalachians, a more ancient mountain chain, flank eastern North America, reaching only half the height of its western counterpart. The vast area between the Appalachians and the Rockies includes the glaciated Canadian Shield to the north, the Great Plains in mid-continent, and the Mississippi basin to the south.

South America has more or less the shape of a triangle. The majority of its 6,900,000 square miles (17,800,000 sq. km) lies close to the equator. Its most important geographical feature is the Andes Mountains, the series of mountain chains that runs uninterrupted from northern Venezuela and Colombia all the way to the island tip of Patagonia. Several mountain peaks reach heights of more than 20,000 feet (6,100 meters). The highest peak is Alconcagua at almost 23,000 feet (7,000 m) tall.

Depending on the altitude and the amount of rain, South America's vegetation varies. A dense equatorial forest stretches along the Amazon River and its tributaries, surrounded by wide bands of savanna. A semiarid region in northeastern Brazil is dotted with cactus. Wooded areas are found farther south. Prairies and steppes are common in the lower regions of Uruguay and Argentina; subantarctic forests are found in southern Chile.

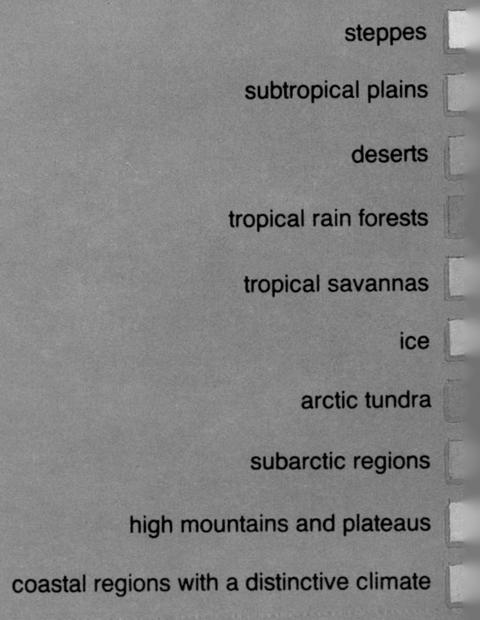

steppes

subtropical plains

deserts

tropical rain forests

tropical savannas

ice

arctic tundra

subarctic regions

high mountains and plateaus

coastal regions with a distinctive climate

GREENLAND

A.D. 1020

NEWFOUNDLAND

The first Europeans to set foot on American territory were the Vikings who arrived in the tenth century A.D. in Greenland and then, around 1020, in Newfoundland.

ATLANTIC OCEAN

A.D. 1492

The last discovery of America was that of the Spanish expedition led by Christopher Columbus, who arrived in 1492 at the island of San Salvador in the Bahamas.

SOUTH AMERICA

Cape Horn

THE DISCOVERY AND SETTLEMENT OF AMERICA

Who Really Discovered America?

The New World has been discovered at least three times. The most celebrated "discovery" is granted to Christopher Columbus, who landed on San Salvador October 12, 1492. The name *Indian* was coined by Columbus who mistakenly thought he had reached the East Indies. But Columbus was really a latecomer to the New World. Five hundred years earlier, Norsemen, or Vikings, from Greenland had sailed the waters of North America, shipping its timber back to their tree-barren homeland.

During the Viking Age, the northern hemisphere was enjoying warm temperatures for the second time since the end of the Pleistocene epoch. Warming seas encouraged Norse explorers to leave traditional coastal routes and strike out across uncharted open water. Some Viking groups expanded westward from their original homes in Scandinavia. By A.D. 870, Norse migrants formed a steady stream into Iceland.

Fifty years later, their Icelandic settlements numbered over thirty thousand individuals.

One Viking, Eric the Red, began exploring unknown coastlines even farther west. In doing this, he discovered a harsh, unpopulated land, with plentiful game hidden in its mountain valleys. Dubbing the place "Greenland"—no doubt to enhance the image of his new find—Eric returned to recruit settlers for this new land.

According to a saga of the Greenlanders, one boatload of Icelandic merchants was blown off course to the southwest, where they spied a wooded coastline with low hills. When this boat finally made its way back to Iceland, the son of Eric the Red—young Leif Eriksson—vowed to return to this new-found land. Eriksson did return. About 1000, he and his crew landed on the eastern coast of North America, which they dubbed Vinland. The Vikings occupied a colony there for about three decades before retreating from the Indians.

The Native Americans

The first human footprint on New World soil belongs to aboriginal people—American Indians and the closely related Eskimos. In the Americas, human beings did not evolve from lower human forms. People migrated into this New World as fully evolved *Homo sapiens*.

Because New World aborigines entered as *Homo sapiens*, they brought with them a cultural heritage. Certain basic skills, such as tool-making, flint-chipping, and the means to obtain food, shelter, and clothing, also came with the first Americans. These early immigrants must also have brought with them a basic social organization, as well as beliefs about magic and the supernatural. They certainly also possessed forms of language. When Columbus arrived, Native Americans of Alaska, Canada, and the United States spoke about two thousand different languages.

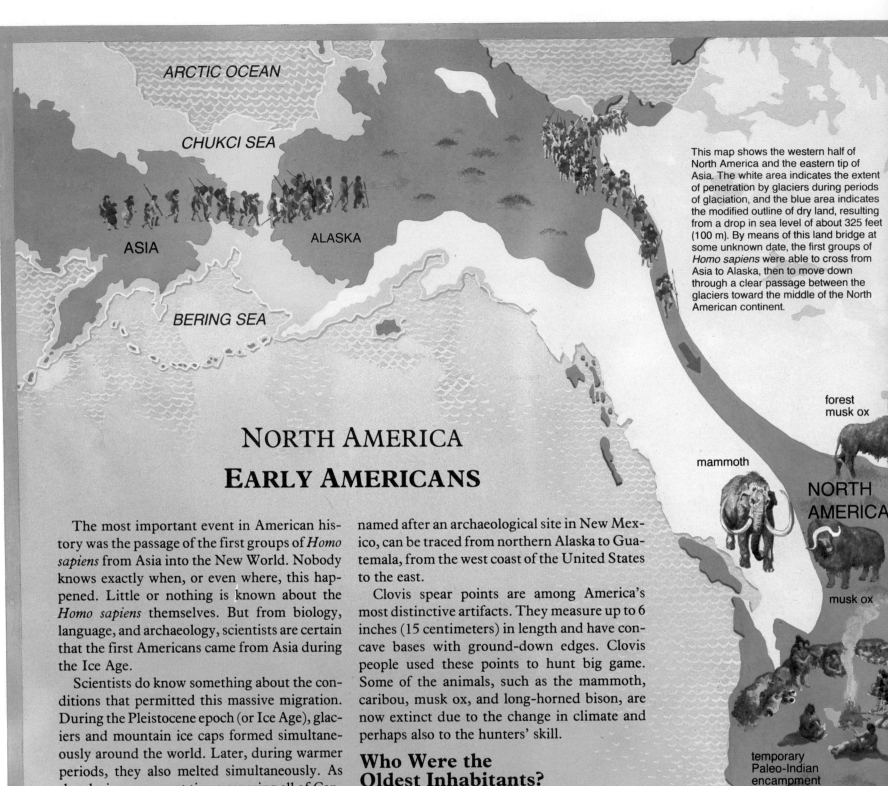

ARCTIC OCEAN

CHUKCI SEA

ASIA

ALASKA

BERING SEA

This map shows the western half of North America and the eastern tip of Asia. The white area indicates the extent of penetration by glaciers during periods of glaciation, and the blue area indicates the modified outline of dry land, resulting from a drop in sea level of about 325 feet (100 m). By means of this land bridge at some unknown date, the first groups of *Homo sapiens* were able to cross from Asia to Alaska, then to move down through a clear passage between the glaciers toward the middle of the North American continent.

forest musk ox

mammoth

NORTH AMERICA

musk ox

temporary Paleo-Indian encampment

camel

PACIFIC OCEAN

CALIFORN

NORTH AMERICA
EARLY AMERICANS

The most important event in American history was the passage of the first groups of *Homo sapiens* from Asia into the New World. Nobody knows exactly when, or even where, this happened. Little or nothing is known about the *Homo sapiens* themselves. But from biology, language, and archaeology, scientists are certain that the first Americans came from Asia during the Ice Age.

Scientists do know something about the conditions that permitted this massive migration. During the Pleistocene epoch (or Ice Age), glaciers and mountain ice caps formed simultaneously around the world. Later, during warmer periods, they also melted simultaneously. As the glaciers grew—at times covering all of Canada to a depth of perhaps 2 miles (3 km)—the sea levels dropped as much as 325 feet (100 m). The dropping sea levels changed the earth's appearance. The Bering and Chukci seas retreated to form a land bridge over 1,240 miles (2,000 km) wide at its maximum. This vast land bridge allowed east Asians to cross into a new world.

The Clovis Culture (10,000-9,000 B.C.)

People were definitely established in the New World before 10,000 B.C. The Clovis culture, named after an archaeological site in New Mexico, can be traced from northern Alaska to Guatemala, from the west coast of the United States to the east.

Clovis spear points are among America's most distinctive artifacts. They measure up to 6 inches (15 centimeters) in length and have concave bases with ground-down edges. Clovis people used these points to hunt big game. Some of the animals, such as the mammoth, caribou, musk ox, and long-horned bison, are now extinct due to the change in climate and perhaps also to the hunters' skill.

Who Were the Oldest Inhabitants?

Clovis is the first well-documented human population to appear in the Western Hemisphere. Despite decades of research, there is no positive proof of a pre-Clovis people in North America. Some scholars believe that humans reached North America between 70,000 and 20,000 B.C—long before the Clovis people. They believe that the many different types of spear points dating from between 10,000 and 8000 B.C are evidence of this. Such a variety would be impossible if the first migration of people had come from Asia only a couple of thousand years earlier.

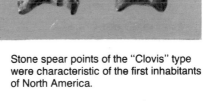

Stone spear points of the "Clovis" type were characteristic of the first inhabitants of North America.

A group of hunters has succeeded in trapping a mammoth in a marshy area and is attacking it with spears and stones.

The C...

As migrating people spread over the New World, they were forced to adapt to many different environments, from interior subarctic to coast tropical. The cultures that developed within these settlements were also affected by the environmental differences. The variety of both settlements and cultures that existed by about 10,000 B.C. can also be used as evidence that people existed in North America much earlier than this. At Meadowcroft Shelter (near Pittsburgh, Pennsylvania), archaeologists discovered evidence of a culture that existed from about 17,000 B.C. The oldest stone artifacts appear to date between 13,000 and 12,000 B.C.

But the archaeology of Meadowcroft Shelter leaves many questions unanswered. The stone tools found there are few, small, and look just like later artifacts. Also, large animals from the glacial age are missing from Meadowcroft Shelter, and this is surprising for a site so old. The vegetation found throughout the rock layers at Meadowcroft also raises questions. The plants are like those found in a mild climate. This is unusual since during part of this time the front of the glacier mass was less than 46 miles (75 km) to the north.

This map shows the northwestern region. The coast is in blue; the interior plateau is in yellow.

A group of coastal Indians navigates an ocean-going canoe. Carved from a single tree trunk, the canoe is about 65 feet (20 m) long.

THE NORTHWEST COAST

America's Northwest Coast extends along the Pacific Ocean from Yakutat Bay in southern Alaska to the Humboldt Bay in northern California. This coastline is cut by a network of channels and fjords, with thousands of islands, large and small. The warm Japanese Current, which flows southward along the coast from Alaska, created a moderate climate with heavy rainfall.

The earliest cultural remains from southeastern Alaska, British Columbia, Washington, and Oregon show no major differences between coastal and interior communities. But such differences developed through time, leading to rather different adaptations. While hunters and river fishers populated the inland, the groups settled along the Northwest Coast underwent

rapid development. Although agriculture was never practiced here and ceramics were unknown, Northwest Coast populations are well-known for their large numbers, rich ceremonies, and for the importance they attached to property, rank, and personal pride.

The Way of Life Changes on the Northwest Coast

On the Northwest Coast, population increased greatly between 2000 and 1000 B.C. Sometime thereafter there emerged a single life-style, which was adapted along the coast both by people to the north and to the south. This life-style used marine resources and relied on a mountainous interior rich in fish and game to achieve the "culture of abundance" that

impressed the earliest European explorers.

Large villages were invariably located at the water's edge on a beach convenient for landing canoes. However, traces of smaller, special purpose sites also remain, suggesting the development of local differences. In the north houses were nearly square and 32 to 65 feet (10 to 20 m) across. They also had vertical side planking and gabled roofs. Sometimes a house had terraced sides, with the cooking fire located on the lower level and sleeping areas on the upper levels. In the south, houses were long and narrow, and occupied by several families, each with its own fire. One such house was nearly 500 feet (150 m) long and 65 feet (20 m) wide. Large wooden houses have been constructed on the Northwest Coast for more than three thousand years, probably indicating the expansion of family organization.

Artifacts became increasingly diverse, particularly after 1500 B.C. Stone artifacts such as mauls, cutting tools, and bowls became common. Bone, shell, and wooden tools were abundant. Woodworking was highly developed on the Northwest Coast; houses, canoes, bowls, spoons, boxes, drums, and masks were carved

wooden
sculpture

The ground plan *(left)* and cross section *(immediately below)* show the detail of a half-buried dwelling at Surprise Valley between 4000 and 3000 B.C. The holes left by the poles and the location of the central fireplace can be seen on the ground plan. The cross section shows the entrance ramp.

On the right: A circular pithouse, with a central fireplace, is half buried in the ground. Its covering is supported by poles and completed with matting. Two women are pounding cereals in a stone mortar, while some men have tanned pelts and are stretching them out to dry.

with symbolic and artistic patterns.

Life on the Plateaus of the Interior

A hunting tradition developed on the interior plateau by at least 8000 B.C. Elk, deer, antelope, beavers, rabbits, and rodents were all favored prey. Two thousand years later, this list broadened to include salmon and river mollusks. Most sites cluster near major rivers, and there is little evidence of upland exploitation.

The interior people—those living away from the coasts—began to live in villages of deeply excavated houses called pithouses. Some of these exceeded 65 feet (20 m) in diameter. In historic times, up to twenty-five people wintered in one house. Equipped with a central fireplace, these houses were mat or bark covered.

Interior people created thousands of stone carvings called petroglyphs. Even today, many cliff faces and boulders are covered with drawings of people, mountain sheep, deer, elk, salmon, beavers, and even imaginary animals. Some petroglyphs tell a story while others seem to be connected with death rites, and a few appear to be tribal symbols.

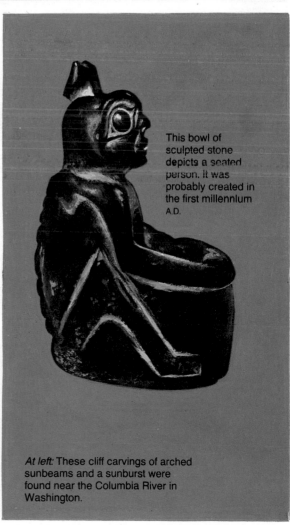

This bowl of sculpted stone depicts a seated person. It was probably created in the first millennium A.D.

At left: These cliff carvings of arched sunbeams and a sunburst were found near the Columbia River in Washington.

11

ANCIENT PEOPLE AND EARLY FARMERS IN THE AMERICAN SOUTHWEST

Paleo-Indians and Archaic (or Desert) People

The earliest human inhabitants of the Southwest were Paleo-Indians of the late Pleistocene epoch (ten to fifteen thousand years ago). They were skilled hunters and lived off now-extinct species of elephant, bison, camel, and horse that roamed the region during that cool, wet period.

The shift toward a warm, dry climate, much like that of the present-day Southwest, began about nine thousand years ago. This shift caused dramatic changes in animal and plant populations. The people who adapted to these conditions were the Archaic or Desert people. These people relied on harvesting wild plants and hunting small animals. Human populations increased during this period, and a variety of cultural artifacts recovered from dry caves throughout the Southwest testify to their skill in textile and basketry crafts. About two thousand years ago, some Desert people of southern Arizona and New Mexico took on a life-style based on the cultivation of maize, beans, and squash.

Early Agriculture

Many early farming cultures have been identified in the Southwest. The best known of these are the Hohokam (of the low deserts of south-central Arizona), the mountain-dwelling Mogollon (of central and southern Arizona and New Mexico), and the Anasazi (of the Four Corners region that includes northwestern New Mexico, southwestern Colorado, southeastern Utah, and northeastern Arizona). None of these people had domestic animals other than dogs and turkeys, nor did any have a written language. Knowledge of them comes mainly through archaeological record.

The Hohokam

The best-known Hohokam village is called Snaketown, located near the modern city of Phoenix in Arizona. It may have been occupied as early as 300 B.C. and abandoned about A.D. 1300. Excavations there document the evolution of Hohokam society. Archaeologists organ-

ize this society into four major periods called the Pioneer period (about 300 B.C.-A.D. 500), the Colonial period (about A.D. 500-900), the Sedentary period (about A.D. 900-1100), and the Classic period (about A.D. 1100-1500).

Pioneer people lived in small villages of wattle and daub houses and built many miles of irrigation canals to water their fields in the low desert country. Weaving, pottery, and shell jewelry were important household crafts. During the Colonial period, populations increased and new communities were established in the mountains and plateaus of central and eastern Arizona. Hohokam society became more complex and crafts more sophisticated. During the Sedentary and Classic periods, villages became larger, but Hohokam territory shrank. In some Classic period communities, thick-walled, multistoried adobe houses were built, and high walls surrounded the villages.

Hohokam ritual architecture included large community houses, ball courts similar to those

12

On the left, above: Shown is a reconstruction of the Hohokam settlement in Casagrande, Arizona. The building of the settlement is made of bricks of hardened earth and wood. It required the excavation of massive amounts of earth and the transportation of lumber from mountains over 50 miles (80 km) away.

1) A piece of Hohokam pottery was found in Snaketown, Arizona, 1000-1100 B.C. 2) This drawing of a turkey was taken from a piece of Mimbres pottery that dates from A.D. 1100-1300. The turkey and the dog were the only domesticated animals. 3) Shown is a splendid example of Mimbres pottery.

On the left, below: The life of the Hohokam people was based on agriculture, especially on maize cultivation, which was made possible by an effective system of irrigation.

A group of Hohokam works with crude tools to maintain a canal that brings water for irrigation from mountains to fields.

found throughout Mesoamerica, and truncated pyramids used as dance plazas or as temple platforms. Other evidence of contact between the Hohokam and the cultures of Mexico include pyrite mirrors and copper bells found at Hohokam sites.

The Mogollon

Mogollon people of the mountains and deserts of southern New Mexico and Arizona are thought to be descended from Desert people who had lived in the region for thousands of years. Their life-styles are characterized by great variety due to the varied environment in which they lived. Generally, their small villages contained pithouses, and their pottery was usually unpainted redware.

Several major Mogollon subgroups have been described. The best known of these is the Mimbres branch of southwestern New Mexico who made remarkable black-and-white painted pottery that was ritually "killed" and buried with their dead. Strong Anasazi influences affected northern Mogollon peoples after about A.D. 1050, and for reasons not well understood, most Mogollon villages were abandoned and the people scattered.

THE ANASAZI

The Anasazi are among the best-known prehistoric southwestern cultures. Their name comes from a Navajo Indian word meaning "the Ancient Ones," and it describes a successful way of life that was shared by many different peoples. The modern Pueblo Indian tribes living along the southern, eastern, and western margins of the San Juan Basin are descendants of the Anasazi. Their history is subdivided into the following periods (and approximate dates): Basketmaker (A.D. 200-700), Pueblo I and Pueblo II (A.D. 700-1050), Pueblo III (A.D. 1050-1300), Pueblo IV (A.D. 1300-1700), and Pueblo V (A.D. 1700-the present).

Early Pueblo Life

The period from Basketmaker through Pueblo II saw a gradual evolution of the Anasazi way of life. Basketmaker people cultivated maize, beans, and squash, hunted, and gathered wild vegetables. Their white or gray pottery was often decorated with black paint. Early Basketmaker people lived in the Rio Grande Valley. Their pithouses resembled those of the Mogollon people.

Pueblo I and Pueblo II people built aboveground houses with connecting rooms. South-facing rock shelters in narrow canyons were favored building sites. Because ceremony was important, most villages were built around a dance plaza and ritual structures called kivas which resembled old-style pithouses. Pottery decoration became more complex, and regional styles developed. The bow and arrow and loom-woven cotton textiles were introduced.

The Classic Pueblo Period

By the time of the Pueblo III, or Classic Pueblo period, the Anasazi dwellings had taken on the well-known pueblo look. During this period, the village populations increased, although actual territory decreased as people moved into the huge pueblo structures. Some of these had hundreds of connecting rooms.

Some pueblos, such as the one in Mesa Verde, were great houses built on cliffs. Others were huge, apartment-like structures like that of the Chaco Canyon. This narrow, dry valley became an early center for Pueblo III culture. Hundreds of miles of roads terminated there, linking it to about one hundred separate communities built in the unique Chacoan architectural style. That style is characterized by fine masonry used to build houses that were several stories high. These houses were terraced to take advantage of solar energy.

Pueblo Bonito at Chaco Canyon with more than eight hundred rooms was the largest of the Chaco great houses. Built in three major episodes between about A.D. 950 and 1130, it still stands four stories high and may once have had a fifth level. Within nine miles of it are a dozen similar buildings as well as many smaller villages. Together, these may have housed as many as six thousand people.

Chaco Canyon appears to have been the center of a complex economic, ritual, and political system. But for reasons that are unclear, the Chaco system ended in about A.D. 1150. During the remainder of the Pueblo III era, Anasazi culture centered in the less dry Mesa Verde area. During the thirteenth and fourteenth centuries, the Anasazi moved into the sparsely populated Rio Grande Valley.

The Late Prehistoric Period

The collapse of the Chaco system was among the first of many such events during the two centuries following A.D. 1150. By the time the first Europeans arrived in the 1530s, the Anasazi people had gained new stability. As many as 50,000 to 100,000 Anasazi people (called Pueblos by the Spanish explorers) were living in more than one hundred towns and smaller villages in New Mexico and Arizona.

All the Anasazi towns and villages had similar economic, political, social, and ritual systems, but they spoke at least six different languages. They held loose alliances with one another but were organized as independent yet equal communities based on farming. Their governments were theocratic, which means that the people believed their leaders to be divinely guided, but all community members were active in ritual life.

Most Pueblo villages were of multi-storied, terraced buildings with hundreds of rooms arranged around plazas. Although they had settled in a new territory, these late Anasazi people were still quite similar to their San Juan Basin ancestors.

A Pueblo Indian uses the typical means to carry liquids or bulk materials.

Large-scale view, above: This reconstruction shows the nucleus of Pueblo Bonito as it must have appeared about A.D. 1000. The work is imposing: dwellings are arranged on four levels around the outer wall; all the circular structures with access ladders in the middle indicate the presence of a kiva or ceremonial room.

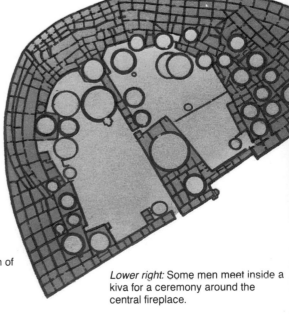

Depicted is a plan of the nucleus of Pueblo Bonito.

Lower right: Some men meet inside a kiva for a ceremony around the central fireplace.

Th
do
go

15

THE NORTHEAST WOODLAND

The Eastern Paleo-Indian Tradition (9000-8000 B.C.)

Meadowcroft Shelter is the oldest, well-documented archaeological site in North America. Yet Meadowcroft remains an isolated case. Widespread traces were left in the Northeast by hunters using fluted-point spears. These hunters had apparently moved in from the south. By 10,000 B.C., the plant and animal life in the Ohio Valley and farther north into Wisconsin, Michigan, and Ontario was plentiful enough to support scattered bands of hunters. The tool forms found throughout the Northeast were all very similar. The widespread similarity suggests that a basic toolmaking ability may have

a distinctive method of working copper. Large and abundant copper nuggets were found on the surface of rock outcrops and in glacial deposits, especially in the Lake Superior area. These nuggets were worked by cold- and hot-hammering methods into spears, knives, ulus, adzes, celts, gouges, awls, and fishhooks.

The Adena Culture (1000 B.C.)

The Adena culture flourished in present-day Ohio about 1000 B.C. The Adena people are known to have been skilled in pottery-making and other crafts. Their sites also show that they experimented in agriculture but depended on hunting, fishing, and gathering to survive.

ments contained graves, they were mainly used for ceremonies.

Hopewell Culture (300 B.C.-A.D. 200)

The Hopewell culture, which followed the Adena, is also known for its complex burial mounds, particularly in central Ohio. Their sites have many more mounds than the Adena's, but these too are surrounded by embankments. Some of their huge earthworks may have been used for defense, but most were used in ceremony or as burial mounds.

Hopewell tombs were wooden, as in Adena, although they were more complex and had a

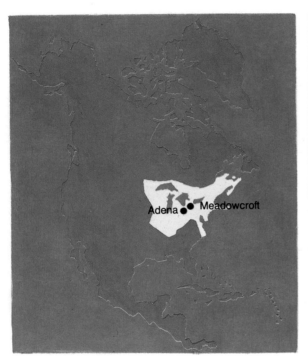

On the map, the yellow indicates the Northeast region.

A cutaway view of the dwelling of the Adena people shows the interior and the fireplace. The reconstruction is based on excavations at Cowan Creek, Ohio.

Two objects from the Adena culture are shown. **1)** The pattern on this terra-cotta vase has been carved into the piece. **2)** This stone-sculptured pipe is an excellent example of the culture's talent. The tobacco was placed in the pipe bowl behind the legs. A hole for the pipe stem was on top of the head.

been adapted to a wide variety of environments, from coastal plain to upland, from river valley to north lakes. Animal bones found in association with these early fluted points are usually woodland caribou, although bones of rodents, deer, and elk are also present.

The Northeastern Archaic People (8000-1000 B.C.)

The Archaic life-style did not spread from a single center. Rather, this life-style appears to have evolved locally at the end of the glacier periods. Existence in the Northeast depended on hunting, fishing, and plant-gathering. Large, broad-bladed dart points and polished-bone tools are characteristic of these people.

After 4000 B.C., these populations developed

But the Adena culture is best known for its mound building. The Adena burial mounds were usually cone-shaped. One of the largest known mounds, Grave Creek Mound in West Virginia, is 65 feet (20 m) high. The mounds were usually simple graves of dirt, stone, and other materials heaped over the dead. But some tombs, such as those of the leaders, were built of timber. These tombs also contained grave goods, or gifts to the dead, such as stone tools.

Around the mounds, the Adena people often built huge enclosures, or embankments. These enclosures were also mounds, and they were often perfectly circular in shape. Some, however, were shaped like animals. The one shown opposite is shaped like a snake and is called the Great Serpent Mound. Although some embank-

series of rooms. Grave goods were more plentiful in these tombs because the Hopewell believed the dead would need things in the next world. Gifts to the dead included ornaments of polished stone or metal, jewelry, pipes, engraved bones, flints, and weapons. The Hopewell sometimes cremated their dead. The bodies were cremated in clay-lined pits, and their ashes were placed in the tombs.

The Hopewell were also skilled in crafts. Copperwork flourished with these people, and small amounts of beaten gold and silver have also been found. Hopewell pottery is mostly cord-marked on the surface.

The Serpent Mound (in Ohio) is about 1,300 feet (400 m) long, 20 feet (6 m) wide, and 5 feet (1.5 m) high. (Inset) An aerial view of the mound shows its complex design.

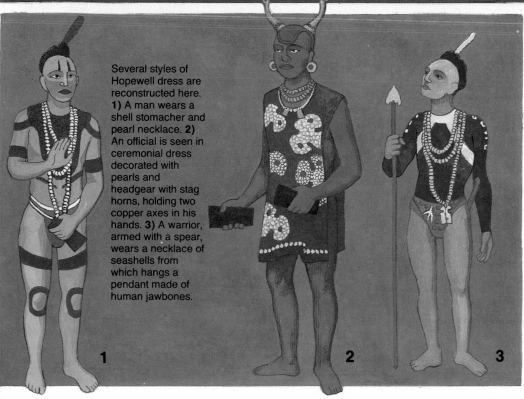

Several styles of Hopewell dress are reconstructed here. 1) A man wears a shell stomacher and pearl necklace. 2) An official is seen in ceremonial dress decorated with pearls and headgear with stag horns, holding two copper axes in his hands. 3) A warrior, armed with a spear, wears a necklace of seashells from which hangs a pendant made of human jawbones.

1   2   3

A Hopewell stone pipe is sculptured in the form of a bird. The mouthpiece is on the left; the pipe bowl is in the bird's back.

This single-colored terra-cotta vase displays decorative carvings.

THE MISSISSIPPIAN PEOPLE

The Eastern Regions in the Late Prehistoric Period (A.D. 700-1540)

Throughout much of the eastern United States, the Late Prehistoric period is characterized by increased dependence upon agricultural products.

The term *Mississippian* describes the highly complex Late Prehistoric societies that thrived along major river valleys of the eastern United States. People living along the Tennessee, Cumberland, and Mississippi rivers made huge earthen mounds and pottery with crushed shell added to temper the clay. Much of the Northeast did not develop in the same way, although people here did achieve some dependence upon agriculture.

Agriculture and the Mississippian Settlements

Agriculture for Mississippian peoples was vastly different from that practiced by European farmers. Because Native Americans lacked domesticated draft animals, agriculture was restricted to hoe cultivation. Because of this, Mississippian agriculture was largely restricted to fertile river valleys.

As these people became more agricultural, centralized authorities became more important. And the more centralized the authorities and population became, the more agriculture became essential for survival.

Mississippian settlements were organized into a specialized social hierarchy. Large, centralized sites with many platform-type mounds functioned as administrative centers. A hierarchy of bureaucrats and priests—from community chiefs, war and peace leaders, and mortuary priests to clan heads—supervised the production, collection, and distribution of foods and materials. They also presided over the city, the construction of mounds and fortifications, and religious and political affairs.

Typical Mississippian towns were planned settlements, with rectangular, single-family houses arranged around an open, central square. The town meeting house, chief's house, and a charnel house were built on adjacent earthen platform mounds. These centers were surrounded by smaller villages, subsidiary farm buildings, hunting or fishing stations, and quarries.

A Special Type of Cult is Born

In the Late Prehistoric period a variety of ritual ceremonies were performed. These rites expressed ancestral obligation, celebrations of successful harvest, hunts and warfare, and burial observances for social leaders.

During the Mississippian period, a special type of cult formed over much of the East. Archaeological evidence of this cult is provided by various objects that began to appear about A.D. 1000, reaching a peak between 1200 and 1400. Called the Southern Cult, this huge network concentrated in three regions: Moundville (Alabama), Etowah (Georgia), and Spiro (Oklahoma). However, the distribution of Southern Cult objects extended beyond the limits of any single Mississippian cultural complex. In addition to small, expensive items, it seems that Southern Cult exchange may have involved subsistence resources such as food. Evidence suggests that the Southern Cult's influence may have extended into the Southeast.

The Decline of the Mississippians

Many of the great Mississippian centers were thriving when the Spaniard De Soto first came to the American Southeast in A.D. 1540. The decline of these Late Prehistoric societies was directly related to European incursions into their territory.

Opposite page, center: The Mississippian settlement at Kincaid, Illinois, was built along the river and included temples, palaces, living quarters, fields, and woods (which provided the people with timber, game, and wild berries).

Opposite page, at top: **1)** A monolithic ax of polished stone comes from Moundville, Alabama. **2)** This cup's handle is shaped like a crested duck. **3)** This vase is in the shape of a human head. *Drawings 5-10:* Representations of animal-gods from the southern cult reflect a high level of skill on the part of the artisans who etched them on copper seashells **(4)**.

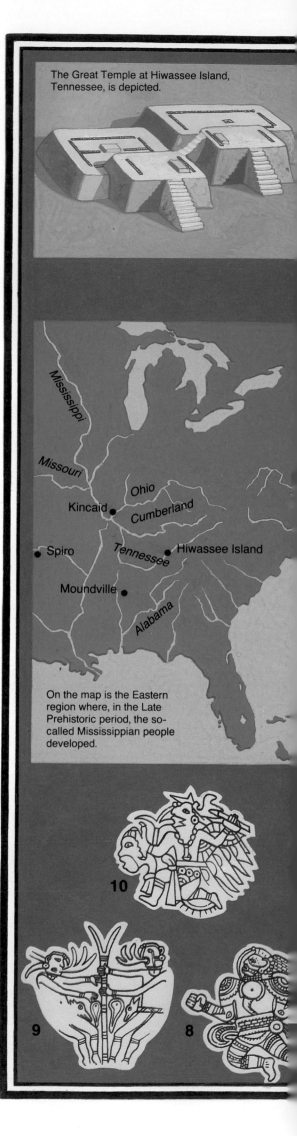

The Great Temple at Hiwassee Island, Tennessee, is depicted.

On the map is the Eastern region where, in the Late Prehistoric period, the so-called Mississippian people developed.

A cross section shows details of one of the Temple Mounds.

1

2

3

4

5

6

7

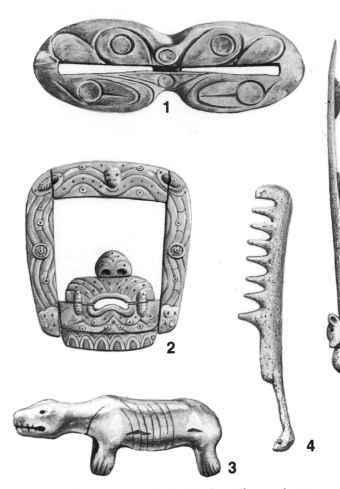

These ivory artifacts come from the Ipiutak culture: **1)** snow glasses; **2)** a sculpture in the form of a mask; **3)** polar bear; **4)** instrument of unknown use; **5)** spear point with stone blades attached.

The Ipiutak hunter, dressed in bear skin and armed with a harpoon, moves toward a seal.

hole for the shaft

head

hole for the string

slit for the stor[e]

Great skill was required to make a bone harpoon: **1)** assembled harpoon, **2)** head, **3)** flexible joint linking head to shaft, **4)** fastener to hold line to shaft, **5)** harpoon parts, and **6)** details of harpoon head.

THE ARCTIC

The Arctic is the vast zone north of the tree-line. Long before Europeans penetrated this foreboding land, each Arctic province had been successfully occupied by Native Americans. Often called Eskimo, they call themselves Inuit, meaning simply "the people." Only the Inuit achieved a successful, year-round adaptation to Arctic conditions without domesticated food resources. Permanent human presence in the Arctic came later than in most other areas of the world.

The Northern Archaic People (4000-2400 B.C.)

The oldest evidence of human occupation dates from between 7000 and 5000 B.C. After about 4000 B.C., the warming climate had stimulated the complete forestation of the Alaskan interior. This resulted in a northward shift of the northern edge of the Canadian forest. These new forests were inhabited by Archaic people. Subsistence methods were similar to those used in more southerly parts of forested continental America. The most important game was caribou. Moose and smaller animals, however, were also being hunted.

In central Canada, a similar northward move-ment had begun by about 6000 B.C., bringing caribou hunters north as they followed the shifting treeline.

The Ancestors of the Inuit Between Tundra and Coast (2000-1000 B.C.)

People of the Arctic Small Tool tradition lived mostly inland, hunting caribou and occasionally visiting the coast to take seals. Surprisingly, there is no solid evidence at this early date that these people hunted seals by cutting holes through the ice—a technique considered indispensable for hunters living permanently on the Arctic coast. These people apparently also lacked boats and dogs. Nevertheless, these

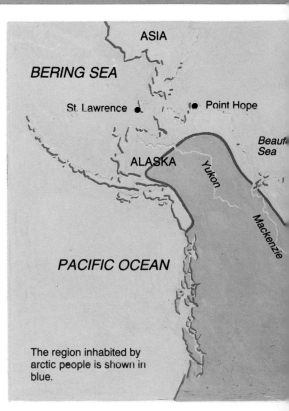

The region inhabited by arctic people is shown in blue.

The hunter sometimes attached inflatable sealskin floats to the end of the harpoon line. The floats and the attached iron ring, which acted as a brake, prevented the seal from escaping beneath the ice.

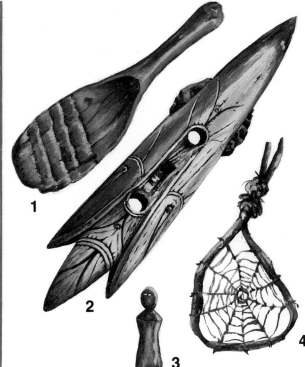

Pictured are artifacts from the Thule culture: **1)** wooden spatula, **2)** harpoon head made from walrus ivory with flint blade inserts, **3)** doll made from bark, **4)** whalebone ladle, and **5)** terra-cotta lamp.

An outside view and a cross section show the details of an igloo—home of the arctic people. The entrance to the igloo is through a door leading into a narrow corridor between two snowbanks.

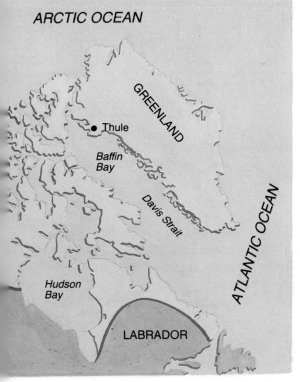

hardy pioneers were the ancestors of modern Inuit people.

The Conquest of the Arctic Coast (1000 B.C.-A.D. 1000)

After a period of apparent depopulation, new groups appeared in the Arctic. In the early years A.D., one of these groups began to take on an appearance of its own. This was the Ipiutak culture, which lasted more than five hundred years. One burial site shows that up to four thousand people lived there in eight hundred log-and-sod houses. Ipiutak people hunted walrus and seal from early spring through summer. In the winter, they moved inland and hunted caribou.

Shallow Ipiutak graves contained small sculptures of walruses, bears, and imaginary animals. Excavations also turned up fine objects carved in spirals and linked chains of ivory. From walrus ivory, the Ipiutak carved harpoon points. From walrus rawhide, they made a line that was the strongest line known before the invention of the steel cable.

The Thule Tradition (100-1800 A.D.)

Sometime around A.D. 1100, the Thule people—immediate ancestors of modern Inuit—spread rapidly throughout northern Canada and Greenland. This was probably due to warmer weather, which changed the path of sea mammal migration. These were the first Americans to make contact with Europeans when the Norsemen arrived in Greenland in A.D. 985.

On the map, in yellow, the subarctic region corresponds to the central belt of present-day Canada.

A cliff painting discovered in Ontario, Canada, depicts men and spotted deer.

THE PEOPLE OF THE SUBARCTIC

Extreme northeastern North America was the "newest" land surface in the New World. It was the last to emerge from beneath the glaciers. Tundra flora rapidly moved into the newly liberated landscape, and various animal species were then drawn into these ecosystems. People did not move into the area until centuries later.

Today, the treeline separating the Arctic from subarctic provides a broad transitional zone. This zone includes tundra and boreal forest. The forested portion is almost impenetrable. Winters in the boreal forest and the tundra are similar. However, summers in the forest are longer and warmer.

The Northern Archaic Period

The first recognizable human activity in the subarctic occurred during the Paleo-Indian period. As the forests shifted farther north, a forest barrier formed between the tundra and the temperate grasslands. That meant that people had various environments in which to live. In this period of continuous change, there emerged a generalized capability to adapt to forest life. This is the so-called Northern Archaic period.

Caribou hunting remained the primary economic activity on the northern fringes of the forest. To the south, moose and deer became mainstays.

During this period, human populations slowly expanded. The number of permanent settlements increased. Also, migratory patterns involved smaller areas, and groups moved from place to place less often. As a result, technological capacities improved and intensified.

A subarctic hunter uses a bow-drill made from caribou antlers. The rotary motion of the point is produced by making the band run back and forth across the shaft.

Caribou hunters, wearing animal pelts and antlers to camouflage themselves, approach a group of caribou.

A cliff painting in Ontario, Canada, depicts a moose, some men in a canoe, and a horned water snake.

Groups of caribou hunters settled in the area round Hudson Bay. Many caribou-hunting sites have been found along the rivers and lakes that lay across the migratory paths of the herds.

The stone implements found in these sites were designed for hunting and killing, skinning and butchering, cutting and splitting bone, and scraping and softening hides. They were also useful in the manufacture of other caribou-related products.

A cold wave hit the region in about 1500 B.C., causing the treeline to shift to the south. Unable to cope with increasingly difficult winter conditions, Archaic people had no choice but to retreat southward. The vacuum left by their withdrawal did not last long, since this same cold period stimulated an expansion of arctic hunters into the interior barrens.

The People of the North Atlantic Coast (4500-1500 B.C.)

During this period, groups of people came to inhabit the Atlantic shores from Labrador to Maine. Many of their archaeological sites are located near deep waters that are exceedingly rich in marine species, especially seals and small whales. Artifacts there show that people hunted marine animals. Also, they were skilled boat-builders and sailors. Because this marine focus was seasonal, the people also depended on traditional land resources.

These people flourished during the first major warm period following the glaciations. Their success waned when cooler conditions set in about 1500 B.C.

MESOAMERICA
EARLY INHABITANTS

Based on historical sources and available archaeological data, the area termed *Mesoamerica* was a region of highly developed culture. In the sixteenth century, its territory was bounded on the north by the Panuco, Lerma, and Sinaloa rivers, and on the south by the Ulua River and the Gulf of Nicoya. Today the territory is divided by archaeologists into various regions or provinces, such as the Central Plateau, the Gulf Coast, Oaxaca, Maya, and Mexican West.

Food Gatherers

In the excavations at Tlapacoya, Mexico, the fossil remains of mastodons, large fowl, and other animals of the Pleistocene epoch were discovered. These findings were associated with tools such as scrapers, razors, and clubs. A fossilized human skull was also found. These remains are among the most recent finds in the Mexican Basin.

From the Teopisca Valley region (Chiapas), a series of tools similar to those of the European Paleolithic period was found. These included hand-held axes, scrapers, and strikers. From a gully at Caulapan (Puebla), comes a scraper dating from around 19,000 B.C. From the Chimalacatlan region (Morelos), come tools and the fossil remains of animals. Traces of ashes, coal, and flint proved that these people knew about fire. The remains of animal bones and plants in several caves are evidence that they used rock shelters and knew how to make basic tools.

Nomadic Hunters

Between 20,000 and 12,000 B.C., people were gatherers of animal and vegetable products. Shortly thereafter they began to use points as weapons. They used the atlatl (or spear thrower) as a weapon in hunting mammoth, the American bison, the giant sloth, the American horse, and other Pleistocene animals. At Santa Isabel Ixtapan, for example, the remains of two mammoths were found. One had traces that showed that it was killed by one point. The second had traces of three points as well as other tools. These hunters ranged over broad areas. They supplemented their diets with gathering. They lived in the open in rudimentary tents in encampments, but they also used caves. They used animal skins for clothing, and they were acquainted with fire and more advanced stoneworking techniques. Several bone and tusk beads indicated that they wore ornaments.

Advanced Gatherers

Climatic changes that occurred between 7000 and 5000 B.C., brought about the extinction of prehistoric fauna. People were forced to depend on woodland vegetables and small game to live. During this phase, people lived mainly on gathered vegetables and lived in the area all year. The people gained knowledge of plant reproductive cycles and of the environmental conditions that best suited the plants. By the end of this stage, people were able to cultivate various species of maize, beans, and peppers. The same period saw the use of the first millstones. There is also evidence of basketmaking, the weaving of hampers, cords, and ropes, as well as coarse cloth, sandals, and mats. The dead were buried in caves and sprinkled with cinnabar or powdered red hematite.

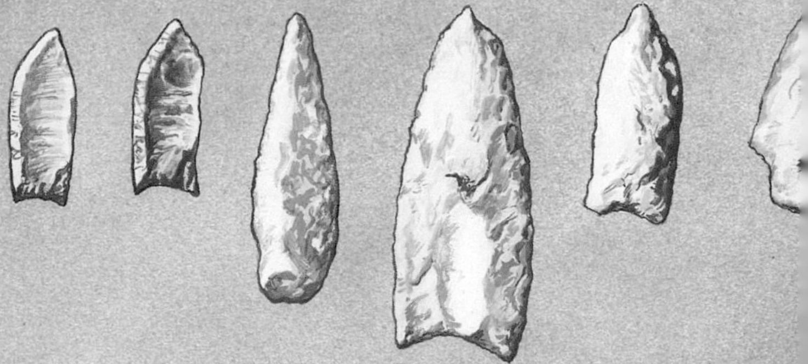

Spearheads used by hunters between 12,000 B.C. and 7000 B.C. are shown.

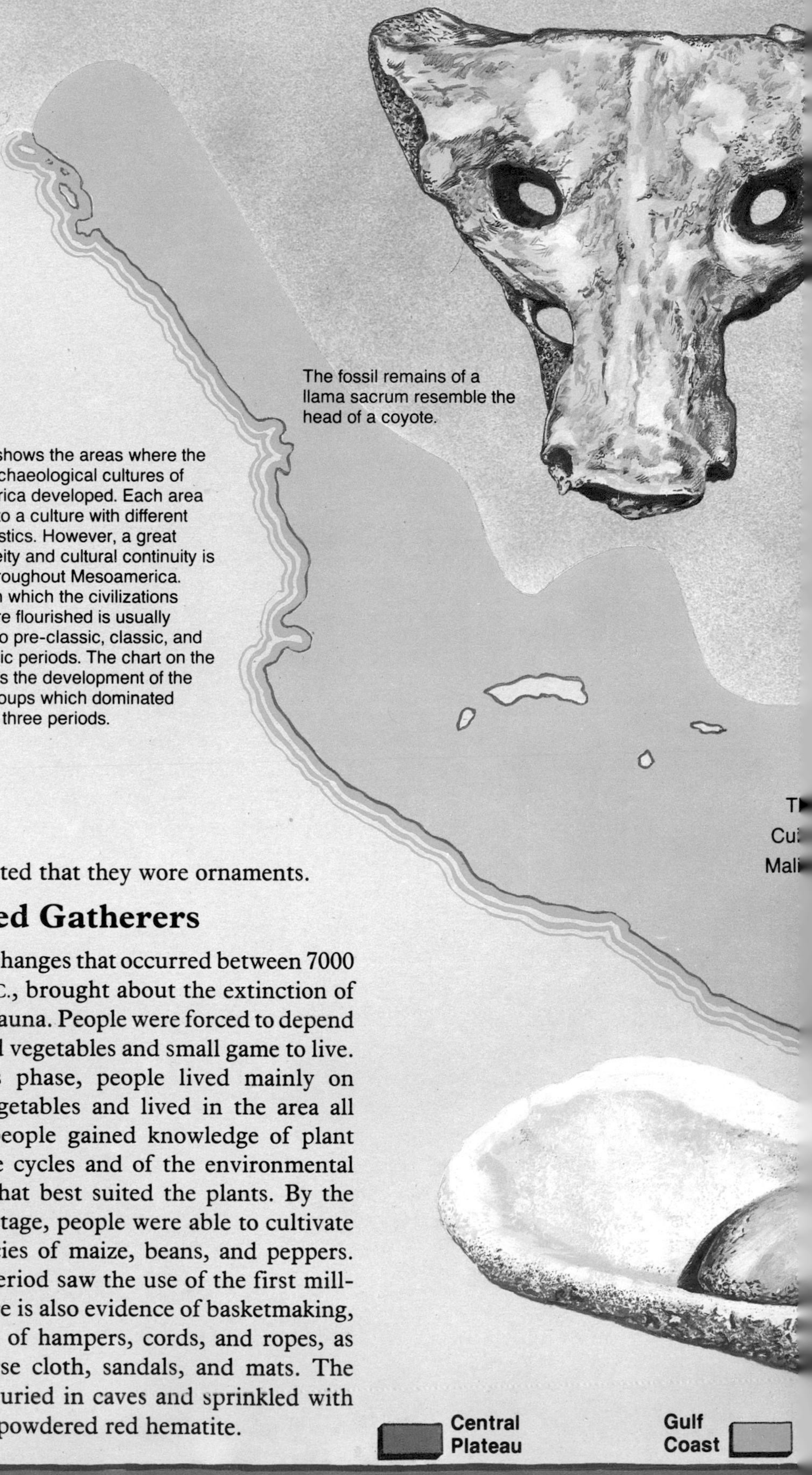

The fossil remains of a llama sacrum resemble the head of a coyote.

The map shows the areas where the various archaeological cultures of Mesoamerica developed. Each area gave rise to a culture with different characteristics. However, a great homogeneity and cultural continuity is evident throughout Mesoamerica. The age in which the civilizations shown here flourished is usually divided into pre-classic, classic, and post-classic periods. The chart on the right shows the development of the various groups which dominated during the three periods.

Central Plateau

Gulf Coast

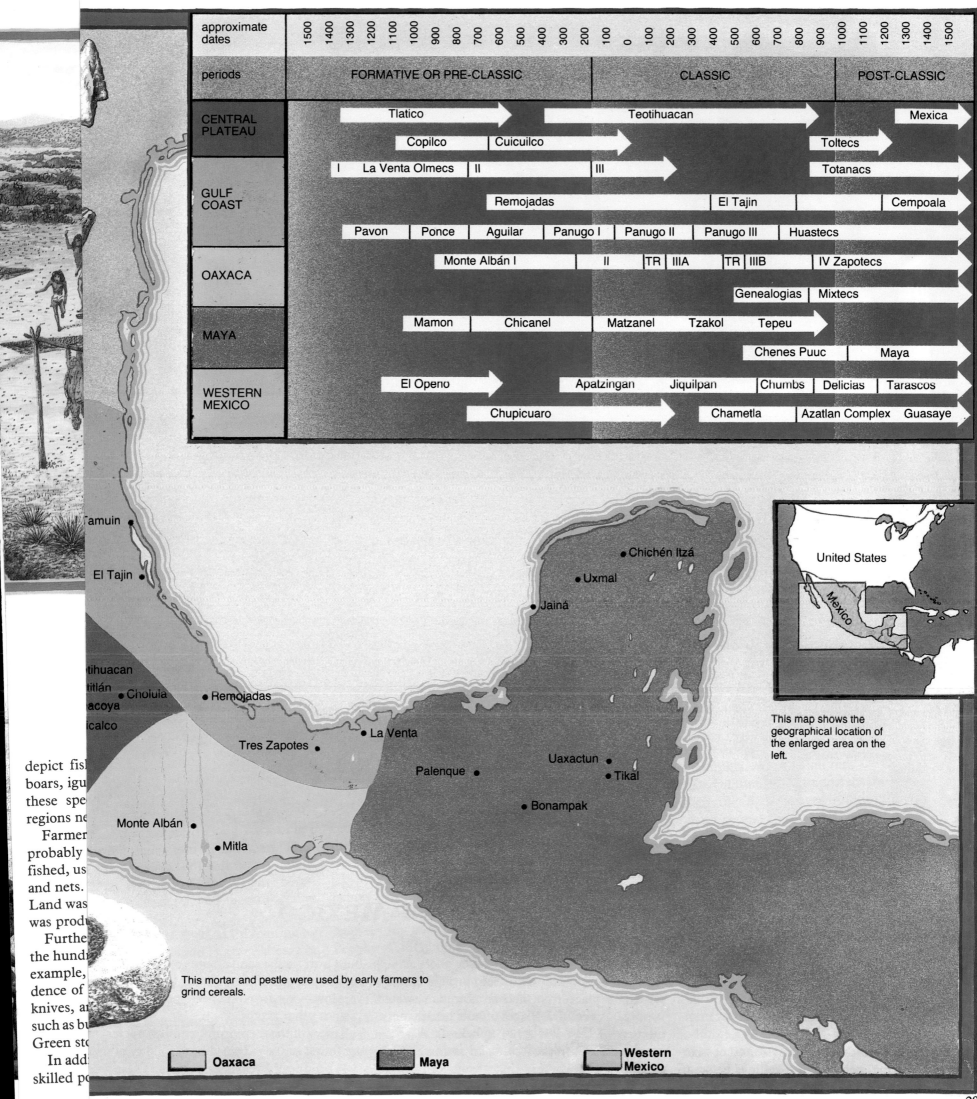

approximate dates	periods
1500 1400 1300 1200 1100 1000 900 800 700 600 500 400 300 200 100 0	FORMATIVE OR PRE-CLASSIC
100 200 300 400 500 600 700 800 900	CLASSIC
1000 1100 1200 1300 1400 1500	POST-CLASSIC

CENTRAL PLATEAU: Tlatico → Teotihuacan → Mexica
Copilco — Cuicuilco → Toltecs →

GULF COAST: I — La Venta Olmecs — II — III → Totanacs →
Remojadas — El Tajin — Cempoala →
Pavon — Ponce — Aguilar — Panugo I — Panugo II — Panugo III — Huastecs →

OAXACA: Monte Albán I — II — TR — IIIA — TR — IIIB — IV Zapotecs →
Genealogias — Mixtecs →

MAYA: Mamon — Chicanel — Matzanel — Tzakol — Tepeu →
Chenes Puuc — Maya →

WESTERN MEXICO: El Openo → Apatzingan — Jiquilpan — Chumbs — Delicias — Tarascos →
Chupicuaro → Chametla — Azatlan Complex — Guasaye →

United States

Mexico

This map shows the geographical location of the enlarged area on the left.

Tamuin

El Tajin

Chichén Itzá

Uxmal

Jainá

...tihuacan
...titlán
Cholula
...acoya
...icalco
Remojadas

La Venta

Uaxactun
Tikal

Palenque

Bonampak

Tres Zapotes

Monte Albán

Mitla

depict fish
boars, igu
these spe
regions ne

Farmer
probably
fished, us
and nets.
Land was
was prod

Furthe
the hundr
example,
dence of
knives, ar
such as bu
Green sto

In add
skilled po

This mortar and pestle were used by early farmers to grind cereals.

| Oaxaca | Maya | Western Mexico |

29

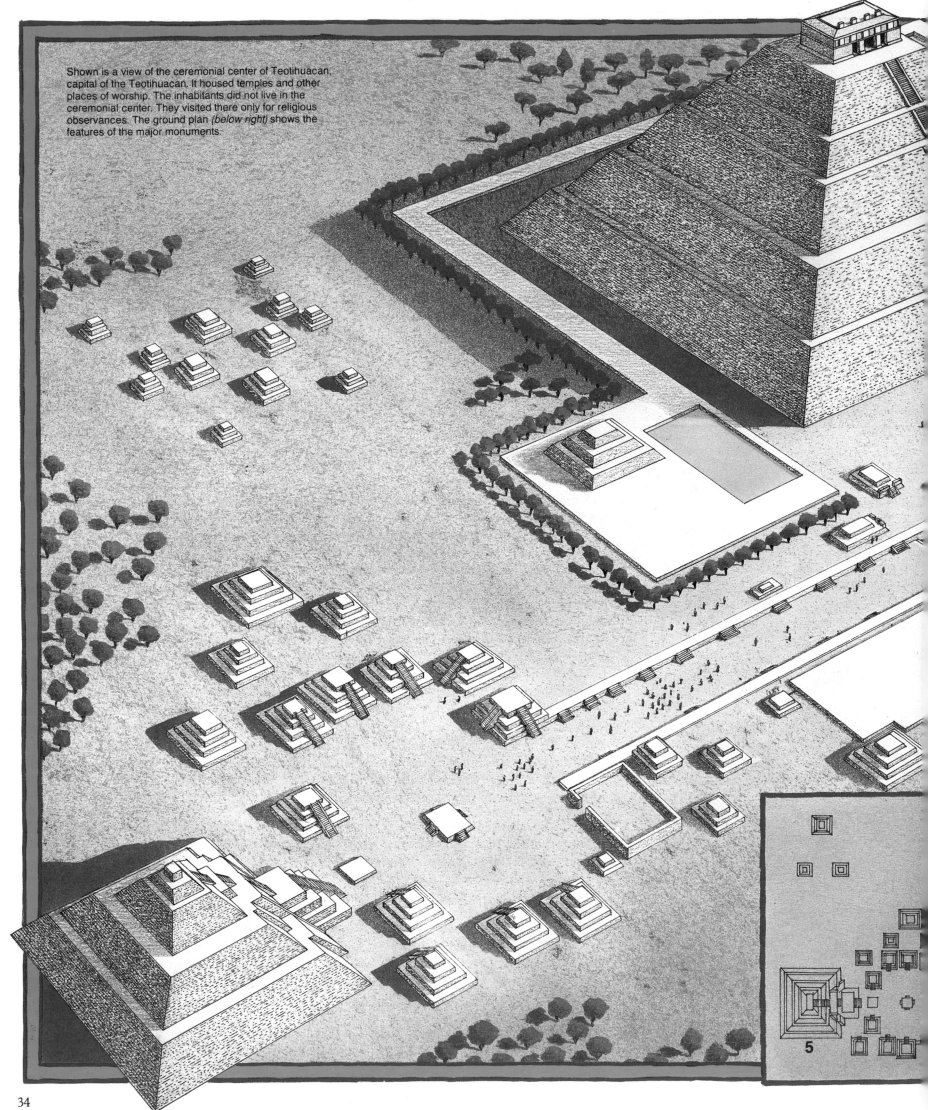

Shown is a view of the ceremonial center of Teotihuacan, capital of the Teotihuacan. It housed temples and other places of worship. The inhabitants did not live in the ceremonial center. They visited there only for religious observances. The ground plan *(below right)* shows the features of the major monuments.

Vil

V
the
The
ing
the
tab

5

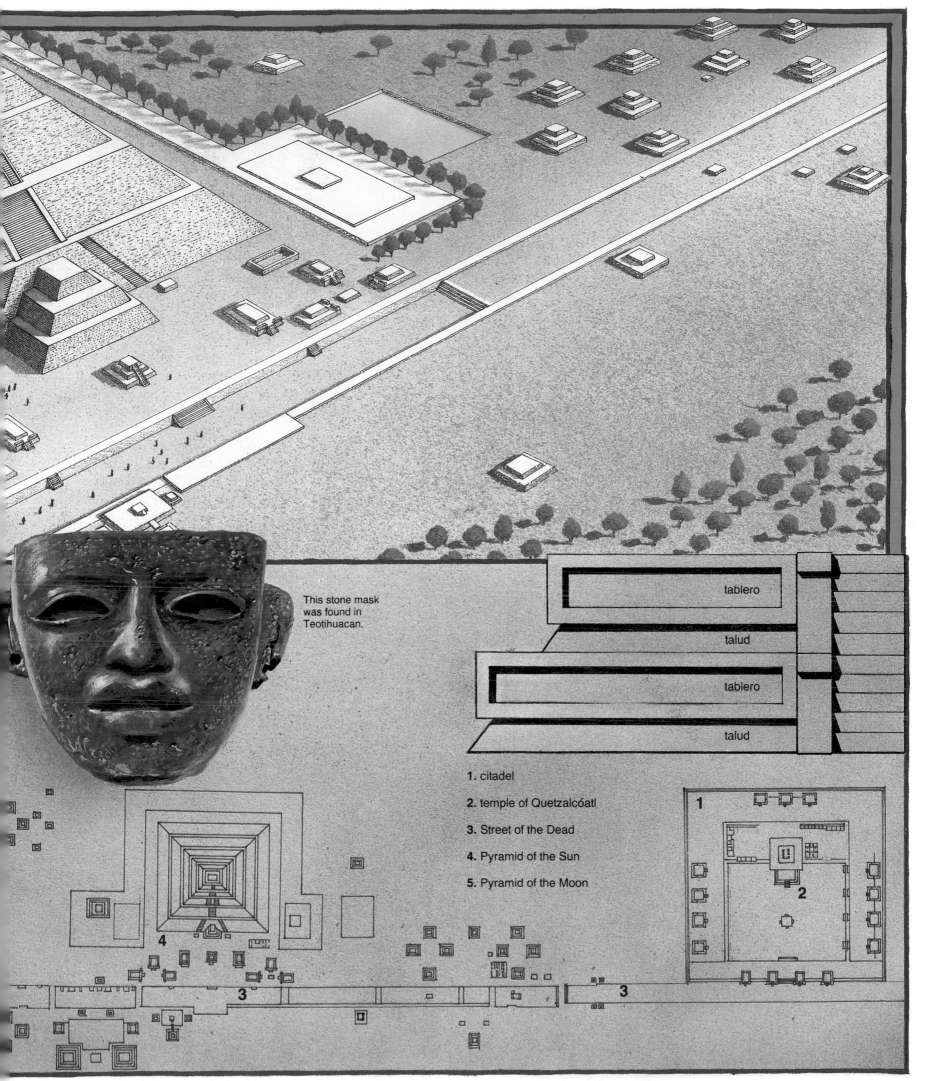

This stone mask was found in Teotihuacan.

tablero

talud

tablero

talud

1. citadel

2. temple of Quetzalcóatl

3. Street of the Dead

4. Pyramid of the Sun

5. Pyramid of the Moon

THE TOLTECS

A People in Search of Land

After the fall of Teotihuacan, many people left the Mexican Basin in search of new land. This was the case with the Toltecs, who moved to Tulancingo for four years and then settled in the area around the river Tula. This became the site of the Tollan Xicocotitlan.

According to the *Annals of Cuauhitlan,* a warrior named Mixcoatl had a son with a woman named Chimalma. The baby was named Ce Acatl Topiltzin (Lord One Cane) with the added title of Quetzalcóatl, the divinity he was supposed to personify.

Acatl grew up in the region of Morelos. When he became an adult, he moved to the lands of Guanajuato and Huasteca. There, the Toltecs rejoined him in order to create the foundations for a kingdom in the city of Tollan, present-day Tula (Hidalgo).

The Toltecs brought together groups of Otoms, Teotihuacans, and Chichimecs. They founded their city at a site between El Corral and the area to the west. Very little is known about the early period of the city's history. More information exists, however, about the period of the highest success of the cult of Quetzalcóatl, under the Mayan influence.

Tula's Apex of Development

During this stage, an enormous plaza with an altar in the center was built. It was reached by a stairway that had decorated friezes on the sides. This stairway was supported by inclined walls.

On one side of the plaza, a great step-pyramid was erected. Nearby, a rectangular structure was constructed adjacent to the major buildings. The most important building was the Temple of Tlahuizcalpantecuhtli. Designs on the structure included motifs of processions of jaguars and coyotes moving in opposite directions, eagles tearing at human hearts, and effigies of the Man-Bird-Serpent, the god Quetzalcóatl.

Not much remains of Tula. The bottom insert shows the present-day ruins of the great ceremonial platform and a possible reconstruction of the upper-level shrine. Several spectacular columns give an idea of the monument's grandeur.

On the upper part there was a temple. Its facade had two columns in the form of serpents, their heads on the bottom and their tails on top. The rest of the temple rested on four rows of columns decorated with images that included warriors, nobles, and earth symbols.

An imposing wall was erected behind this building. It was decorated with halved seashells (symbols of the wind), and it had a large freize in bas-relief. The main motif of the edges has a serpent swallowing a skeletonlike figure.

After the Temple of Tlahuizcalpantecuhtli, the Burnt Palace was built. It had a portico of columns covered with four stone slabs. Inside were altars with a chacmol sculpture and a frieze. The frieze depicts a winding procession of warriors and priests in parade dress. The chacmol are warriors with containers on their stomachs in wait for the human hearts about to be sacrificed.

Warriors and Skilled Artisans

All this information leads to certain clear-cut facts. It is obvious that Quetzalcóatl was worshiped at Tula and that the population included skilled artisans. These included whitewashers, painters, masons, carpenters, plasterers, stone-cutters, and feather-workers. It is also known that during that period there developed the style of the serpentine columns, the chacmol, the bench-lined walls, the columns decorated with images of warriors, and the porticos and colonnades of the type found at various sites in Yucatán.

The dates A.D. 900 and 1168 mark the beginning and end of the history of Tula (Hidalgo). The city prevailed over other less-advanced peoples and formed alliances. Its level of civilization placed it in a position of undisputed power over the other cultures of the Plateau. Tula was believed to be a city of skilled artisans and artists.

After the fall of Tula, some of its people went into exile and with their lord Nauhyotzin settled at Culhuacan, another site in the Mexican Basin.

THE AZTECS

The Mexica were nomadic tribes from the north. They moved to the Mexican Basin, together with other groups who, like themselves, were searching for land. After passing through various areas, including the area around Tula, they reached the Chapultepec region.

Since most of the land was already occupied, the Mexica were almost constantly in battle. To avoid battle, they moved to a small island and there founded their capital, Tenochtitlán, in 1325.

With great effort, they brought materials from the mainland and began the construction of a great metropolis. The city stood as a great cultural, political, and administrative center. It was defended by four walls, which had four gates decorated with serpents. From each gate a road led from the island to the mainland.

The Mexica constructed dams, barriers, and aqueducts to keep the salt water away from the city's water supply. They built public fountains, streets of dirt and wood, and created a vast system of canals. In the center of the city was the Major Temple, a symbol of power. It had two stairways with friezes ending in cubic motifs. The stairs led to two identical temples. One honored the god of rain, the other the god of wars.

Facing the Major Temple was another cone-shaped temple in honor of the god of the wind. Other temples were dedicated to numerous gods. There were also military depots, warehouses, halls for poets and singers, and libraries. Close to the center of the city were the palaces of the governors of Axayacatl and Montezuma.

A Cosmopolitan Center

The economy of the Mexica was based on agriculture and items provided by artisans. The products were usually sold in markets. Economic demand for the products was high, and merchants sold their goods in surrounding areas. These areas extended along the coast as far as Xicalango and also through Puebla and Oaxaca and on into Soconusco.

The greatest demand was for high-quality and exotic goods. These included jade, rock crystals, jewels, bracelets of precious metals, objects made from tortoise shells, plumes from the quetzal bird, and jaguar pelts.

The warrior class had the most power in the city. Second to them were the priests. Their main task was to spread their religion to conquered people. The priests also organized celebrations to honor the gods.

The union of the gods Ometecuhtli and Oecihuatl produced four offspring, the Tezcatlipocas. One of these deities was Quetzalcóatl and another Huitzilopochtli. Other divinities were Huehueteotl, lord of fire; Tlaloc, lord of rain; and Xipe Totec, patron of the spring and products of the earth.

In Tenochtitlán, there were artisans of all sorts, including jewelers, feather-workers, stone-cutters, and illustrators. There were also sculptors, architects, experts in hydraulics, doctors, writers, and poets. Many artisans from other regions came to Tenochtitlán because of the city's splendor.

The map below locates Tenochtitlán and the numerous small regional centers whose life revolved around the capital. This region corresponds to the small rectangle on the map at right.

Xaltocan

Texcoco

Tepevacac

Tlacopan

TENOCHTITLAN

Ixtapalapa

Xochimilco

Cuitlahuac

Mizquic

United States

Mexico

Gulf of Mexico

Pacific Ocean

In the heart of Tenochtitlán, there arose the ceremonial center, a vast four-sided structure measuring 985 feet (300 m) per side. Its double walls contained temples and other ritual buildings, in addition to the emperor's quarters. It was made of square rock blocks and lime, either white or painted in bright colors. The center was dominated by the major temple (1) which stood about 195 feet (60 m) high. A set of 114 steps led up to two small twin-pyramids with statues of Huitzilopochtli, god of war, and Tlaloc, god of rain, adorned with gold and precious stones, whom the Aztecs honored with human sacrifices. The circular temple of the god of the wind rose in front of the major center (2). A little farther on, there rose the site where pelota matches were played (3), and on the right, was the temple of Tezcatlipoca, god of darkness (4). The priests lived in a building with a terraced roof (5). To the south, extended the great palace of Montezuma (6). This reproduction is based on a plastic model in the national Museum of Anthropology in Mexico City.

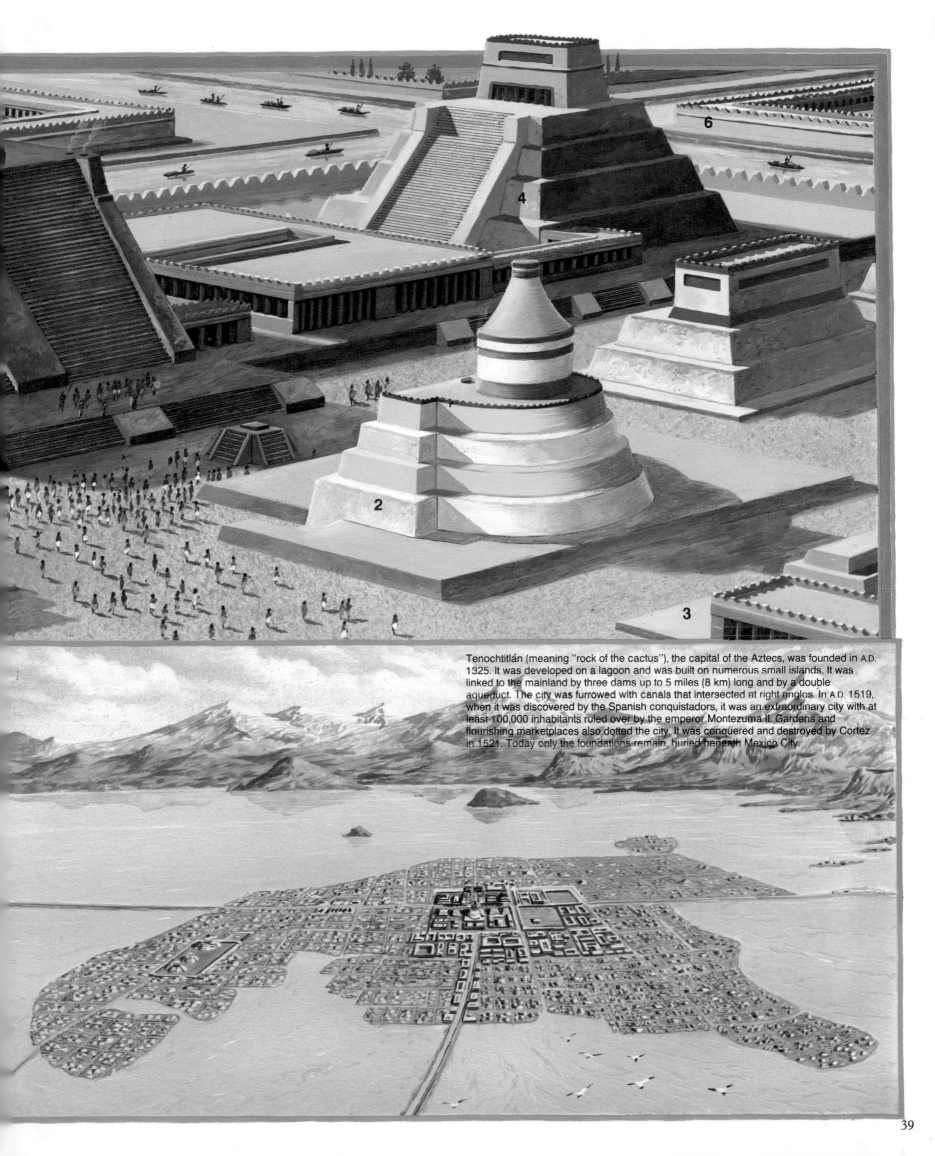

Tenochtitlán (meaning "rock of the cactus"), the capital of the Aztecs, was founded in A.D. 1325. It was developed on a lagoon and was built on numerous small islands. It was linked to the mainland by three dams up to 5 miles (8 km) long and by a double aqueduct. The city was furrowed with canals that intersected at right angles. In A.D. 1519, when it was discovered by the Spanish conquistadors, it was an extraordinary city with at least 100,000 inhabitants ruled over by the emperor Montezuma II. Gardens and flourishing marketplaces also dotted the city. It was conquered and destroyed by Cortez in 1521. Today only the foundations remain, buried beneath Mexico City.

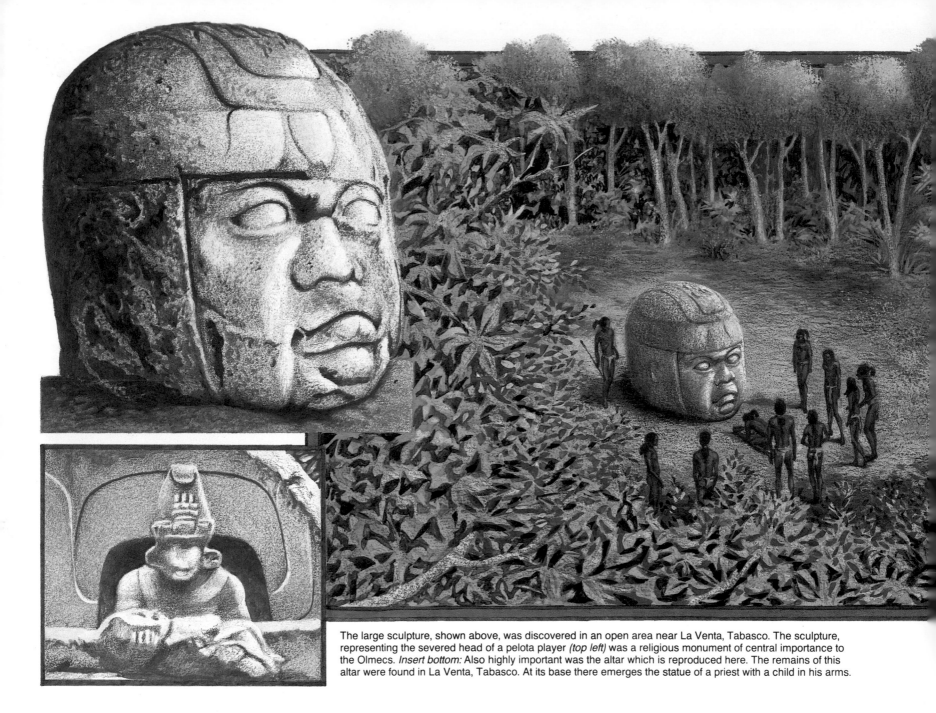

The large sculpture, shown above, was discovered in an open area near La Venta, Tabasco. The sculpture, representing the severed head of a pelota player *(top left)* was a religious monument of central importance to the Olmecs. *Insert bottom:* Also highly important was the altar which is reproduced here. The remains of this altar were found in La Venta, Tabasco. At its base there emerges the statue of a priest with a child in his arms.

THE OLMECS

The Land of Rubber

Mysterious groups of artists seem to have once lived in Los Tuxtlas, the forests south of Vera Cruz, and in the marshes of Tabasco. These groups were called Olmecs. They were from Olman, the land of rubber. Some scholars believe that the Olmecs arrived in small waves from as far south as Ecuador. In any case, some of them made their way as far as Oaxaca, Guerrero, Puebla, Morelos, and the Mexican Basin. Others crossed the Isthmus of Tehuantepec and reached the Gulf Coast. Wherever they went, however, they brought their cultural values.

Around 2400 B.C., their influence led to a tradition of coarse, plain pottery. But around 1700 B.C., there was a rich tradition in decorative motifs: impressions made with cords and fabric, fingernail impressions, and decorations made with combs, for example. These motifs had already been used in Ecuador, Columbia, and other places from about 3000 and 2500 B.C.

The Olmecs introduced other innovations. These included travel by means of rafts and canoes, the construction of pile-dwellings and palisades, and the planting of tubers such as the yucca.

Olmec Villages

From 1700 to 1200 B.C., there was an Olmec village stage marked by the penetration, spreading, and stabilization of Olmec culture within lands that were occupied by other peoples or within lands that were unpopulated. This occurred from Altamira (Chiapas) to Tlatilco in the Mexican Basin, and from Oaxaca to the Gulf Coast.

At Tres Zapotes and San Lorenzo (Veracruz) and at La Venta (Tabasco), archaeologists have found pottery with decorations of the claws, spots, teeth, and eyelashes of the jaguar. Th

This statuette depicts a priest wearing a jaguar pelt on his shoulders. The jaguar was a sacred animal.

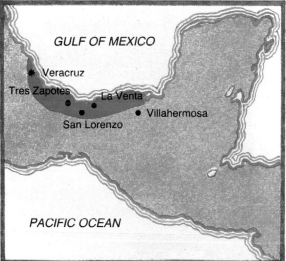

GULF OF MEXICO

* Veracruz

Tres Zapotes • • La Venta
• • • Villahermosa
San Lorenzo

PACIFIC OCEAN

The spread of Olmec artworks is mapped in red.

jaguar was feared and venerated and symbolized earth and fertility. Also at this time, there was a popular type of pottery that was black with a white rim or white with a black rim.

The Olmecs preferred to settle near waterways and forests. During this village stage, the organization of clans flourished, and trade with the Central Plateau prospered.

Religious Centers

The rise and fall of the Olmecs was from about 1200 to 100 B.C. The height of their power coincided with that of a theocracy which initiated the construction of earthen mounds and temples made of clay and straw. Religious centers were also organized. The centers had living quarters, residences for distinguished people, and other structures. Dirt was the only building material used. Attention was also paid to embellishing these sites with sculptures, including huge stone heads. Some of the heads were more than seven feet (two meters) high.

These heads were probably likenesses of victims offerred in sacrifice on the occasion of the pelota games. The heads subsequently served as an element of defense for the community.

The Olmec Culture

Other noteworthy sculptures included great stone containers resembling sarcophagi, sculptures of priests wearing jaguar masks, and floor mosaics of green stones with jaguar heads. The Olmecs also produced axes carved in the form of flower petals, masks, earrings, and necklaces.

The Olmecs also produced a series of statues and headstones, on which there were hieroglyphics and circles with numerical values. This has led scholars to believe that the Olmecs developed a calendar and a counting system. The Olmec expansion affected all of Mesoamerica.

A MAYAN CITY—CHICHÉN ITZÁ

Regional distinctions among Mayan cities can be made on stylistic peculiarities. There was a distinctive Peten style that was characterized by enormous platforms onto which other structures were attached. The structures had high step basements with single-room temples defended by battlements.

The Palenque style, on the other hand, consisted of low structures with smoothly surfaced bases and temples resembling stone huts. Each temple had a corridor and two rooms (portico and sanctuary) on the inside, battlements in the center of the roof, and two external facades decorated with painted figures and motifs of molded plaster.

The Rio Bec style was distinguished by ornamental towers positioned at the ends of elongated buildings. The base-temples had a central gate that was enclosed by gigantic serpent masks.

The Chenes style made use of similar elements, such as large frontal masks consisting of mosaics of plastered stone.

Chichén Itzá means "wells of the Itza." It is a name given to the city after the Spanish conquest. The city is located in a hilly

region of the Yucatán plateau, where there are no rivers. Rainwater, however, filters into the limestone. This water-bearing layer is accessible through large natural wells called cenote. Chichén Itzá was founded in close proximity to two enormous cenote.

The history of the city has become a topic of yet unresolved debate. There has been discussion of an early inhabited center which is supposed to have been invaded in the tenth century either by the Toltecs or by the Maya from the Gulf Coast. A people known as the Itzá is mentioned as an invader both in its own narratives and in Spanish documents. Some scholars identify them with the Toltecs, others with the Maya. Still others have offered the hypothesis that there were several occupations. In any case, it is evident that Chichén Itzá was a powerful center. After the fall of the classical cities, Mayan civilization came to be expressed through the splendor of Chichén Itzá.

A diagram of the center of Chichén Itzá is seen below. Note the Castillo (a nine-step pyramid with staircase and inner temple), the Temple of the Warriors, the Thousand Columns (where perhaps a marketplace was found), and the Nuns Temple (a complex of buildings which appears to have housed both residences and a temple). Nearby stand the two small temples, known as Colorado House and the Caracol, and the ball court. *Also below:* **1)** This sculpture of a half-reclining figure is the Chac Mool, or divine messenger. It comes from the Castillo. With its hands on its stomach, it holds a plate with an offering to the sun. **2)** The eastern face of the Nuns Temple is decorated in Chenes style. **3)** A mosaic disk was found in the sacred cenote.

The Nuns Temple

Caracol

Cenote

Colorado House

Thousand Columns

Castillo

Temple of the Warriors

ball court

sacred cenote

1

2

3

47

The Game of Ball

The most widespread game in Mesoamerica was a ball (or pelote) game that varied greatly in its rules, type of playing field, number of players, and size of the ball. Many playing fields and detailed evidence are to be found in the Veracruz region. The game was played by two teams using a latex ball in an area bounded by two parallel platforms. Spanish chroniclers have told how the game (tlaxtli) was played among the Aztecs. The object was to prevent the ball from entering one's own half of the field. The ball could be hit with the shoulders, forearms, elbows, and hips. Successfully knocking the ball through stone rings on the walls could be of crucial importance to win the game.

The Maya called the game pok-a-tok, but not much is known about it. The playing fields remain, usually in the shape of an "I," marked in the middle and on the sides by stone signals often found at temple sites. It is certain that this game was both a sport and a religious rite. The ball's path symbolized the sun's orbit, and the playing field represented the earth.

VERACRUZ

The Veracruz region extends from the Ca[...] zones River to the Nautla River. Various peo[...] ples had lived in the area. They are referred to a[...] the Veracruz Center cultures. From at leas[...] 1500 B.C. onward, such sites as El Trapiche[...] Chalahuite, and Viejon were active. They pro[...] duced pottery that was richly decorated. Thes[...] people were succeeded by the Remojadas com[...] plex, consisting of a number of farming villages[...] Their products included a red-colored pottery[...]

The second stage of the Remojadas cultur[...] begins with the construction of burial mounds[...] The body of the deceased was placed in th[...] center of the edifice along with funerary offer[...] ings. Everything was then covered over wit[...] earth. These earthen mounds subsequentl[...] came to function as bases for temples and wer[...] eventually organized into complex structures.

Sculpture

The third stage was the high point of th[...] Veracruz Center culture. Groups of people o[...] unknown origin settled in places such as Xiuh[...] tetelco, Quiahuiztlan, and El Tajin. Great citie[...] arose. Architecture was marked by the use o[...] the talud and tablero forms, the latter sur[...] mounted by a light cornice, using brick-size[...] slabs with receding and protruding motifs t[...] form recesses. The recesses were then plastere[...] and painted. The bases, consisting of superim[...] posed sections, had a central stairway wit[...] friezes and recesses along the sides.

Other buildings with elevated talud and ta[...] cornices were decorated with key pattern[...] Enormous slabs had bas-reliefs and scenes fron[...] the pelota game.

In the same period, columns formed by finel[...] carved stone drums, and some minor sculpture[...] called yokes were produced. The yokes seeme[...] to be dedicated to the earth and were burie[...] with beheaded pelota players. Other so-calle[...] palm sculptures, probably inspired by the breast[...] plates worn by the players, and a number o[...] "smiling" clay figurines with large heads, ele[...] gant attire, and a broad, serene smile were als[...] produced.

New Migrations

These groups occupied Papantla, Misantla[...] and other localities in which they are still found[...] Hastened along by invasions of Toltecs an[...] Mexica, other groups that mixed with th[...] preceding ones arrived. One of these was th[...] Totonac group which, after crossing the Zem[...] poala plains, settled at Veracruz, Quiahuiztlan[...] and Boca Andrea.

Totonicapán was situated in the center of the Veracruz region. Its territory was divided into three areas—the plains, the sierra, and the plateau. There were peaks up to 6,500 feet (2000 m) high. Groups of people settled along the rivers or in enclosed valleys. This region included the states of Hidalgo and San Luis Potosi, as well as the Huastesca area of Veracruz.

The Totonacs

Practically speaking, Totonicapán is equivalent to the Gulf Coast. The name means "where maize, the food, abounds." Between A.D. 900 and 1000, the Totonacs had already settled in this region and were beginning to expand.

Their style of architecture was similar to that of the Mexica—two identical temples and a double-stairway with the frieze replaced by tubes. Other buildings had a line of battlements along the top. Plazas were wide.

Potters produced a very refined orange-colored pottery that was decorated with bas-reliefs and painted black. A multicolored pottery also existed. A number of enormous figures of deities were shaped directly from clay mixed with argil and then painted.

Totonicapán was responsible for several innovations in agriculture. These included the use of seedbeds for plant reproduction and the transplanting of crops. Irrigation canals were also used. When the Spaniards reached Zempoala, they were dazzled by the splendor of the dwellings. It was there that the Spaniards came into contact for the first time with the natives of the continent.

Shown is a view of the sacred city of El Tajín (Veracruz). In the foreground is the Pyramid of Niches. The play of light and shade on its decorations produces varied effects.

Pictured are stone reproductions of equipment used by ball players from the Veracruz region. These reproductions were intended for funeral use. On the bottom is a yoke or belt to protect the hips and act as a ball deflector. On the top right is a "palm" in the form of joined hands. This piece was probably used to catch and throw the ball. The tool at left probably represents the head of a player with a dolphin-shaped helmet.

49

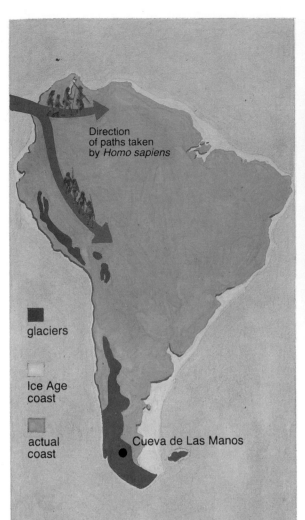

At the end of the Ice Age, hunters armed with spears, clubs, and boleadoras *(in left foreground)* attack a herd of wild horses. The horse would soon become extinct and only reappear after many thousands of years, reintroduced into America by the Europeans.

South America in the Last Ice Age

In South America, glaciers reached their maximum extension by about 17,000 B.C. The narrowing landmass in the south impeded the formation of large ice caps. That took place only in the extreme south. The continental glacier covered all the Magellanico-Fueguian region and the area of the Patagonian Andes up to the thirty-ninth parallel south.

Farther north, the glacier made a limited advance into the High Andean Cordillera, the White Cordillera of Peru, and the Eastern Cordillera in Columbia. Due to the accumulation of ice formed by oceans over the surfaces of both continents, the level of the oceans simultaneously fell, freeing vast sectors of the continental shelf. This phenomenon is found particularly on the Atlantic side of South America. The seas dropped until they were about 500 feet (150 m) below today's level. The glaciers began to retreat about 15,000 B.C. By about 9000 B.C. they had reached their approximate present-day positions.

Scientists are certain that humans did not originate in South America. People must have arrived in small groups of hunter-gatherers across the Central American isthmus, just as their ancestors had crossed the region that today corresponds to the Bering Strait. The earliest evidence of humans dates back to the end of the last glacial period.

SOUTH AMERICA

EARLY INHABITANTS— PALEOLITHIC HUNTERS AND GATHERERS

Primitive Hunters

The dating of the oldest human settlements in South America is largely uncertain. Through modern dating methods, scientists know that by 11,000 B.C. humans had already settled in southern Chile and Patagonia. This means that they must have crossed the more northerly regions of the continent at a much earlier time. Discoveries made in Brazil and in the area of the Andes Mountains seem to confirm the existence in South America of groups of vegetable gatherers and hunters that had primitive stonecutting techniques.

The appearance of stone points indicated a world of superior hunters. This was perhaps the result of a local revolution which occurred at one or more sites on the American continent.

But it may have been a consequence of migratory movements from Siberia. The oldest South American settlements date from about 12,000 B.C. The Taima-Taima site in Venezuela (11,000 B.C.) produced the first foliated stone points, which subsequently spread throughout the Andes region. The Moteverde site, in southern Chile, contained the footprint of a child preserved in clay. At all recorded sites, there are traces of extinct animals especially mastodons and horses. Remains of animals that have survived were also found. These animals were hunted and exploited in various ways by the Paleo-Indians.

Around 9000 B.C., more highly skilled groups of human beings appeared. They could make spearheads according to well-defined models.

The Pinturas River canyon is seen from the heights of Cueva de las Manos. The canyon is known for its "negative" handprints, such as those shown on the left.

Below right: **1)** A skull from Punin, Ecuador, is similar to those from other areas of the Andes, Brazil, and Patagonia. **2)** This double-edged razor found in the Los Toldos Grotto, Patagonia is over ten thousand years old. **3)** Stone points with fishtail stems, or peduncles, were commonly used from 9000-7000 B.C.

Guanacos were common in rock paintings such as this one from Tarata, Peru.

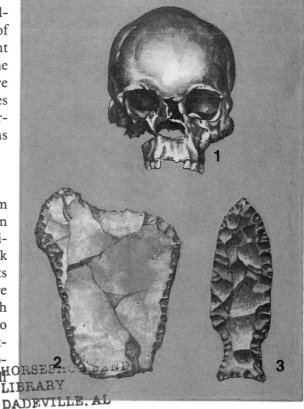

These workers came, as did their predecessors, from the southern tip of the continent. Typical items are projectile points that have an extended base in the form of a fishtail. Some points had a fluting similar to those of the Clovis points found in North America. The communities composing this Paleo-American culture were forced to live together and to hunt the last wild horses of the pampas of Patagonia.

Hunters and Gatherers in the Andes Region

Beginning about 8000 B.C., the Andes region was dominated by a particular type of stone point used for hunting various animals. The groups of this period were not primarily hunters. They were specialized gatherers, capable of living in the various ecological niches in the Andean plateau and valleys. These people often followed the seasonal movements of the animals. Hunting was probably only done in an organized way during the summer in elevated regions.

This intensive hunting and gathering developed in the Andes region over a period of roughly five thousand years. Two important cultural adaptations occurred here. Along the northern and central coast of Chile, there were seafood gatherers and fishers. In the high Andes valleys, there were the migratory hunter-gatherer-planters. Among these people are the origins of American agriculture.

Rock Art

Since it is not possible to date rock art from northern and eastern Brazil, scientists maintain that the Patagonian hunters of the Tolden tradition are responsible for the oldest known rock art in America. These pictures are rich in points and simple geometrical elements. There were also images of guanacos (at times grouped with human figures) and human hands. Llamas also appear in paintings by postglacial Andean hunters. These are found in the vicinity of Laurico-cha and in the extreme southeast of Peru, as well as in other areas of northern Chile.

HORSESHOE BEND LIBRARY DADEVILLE, AL

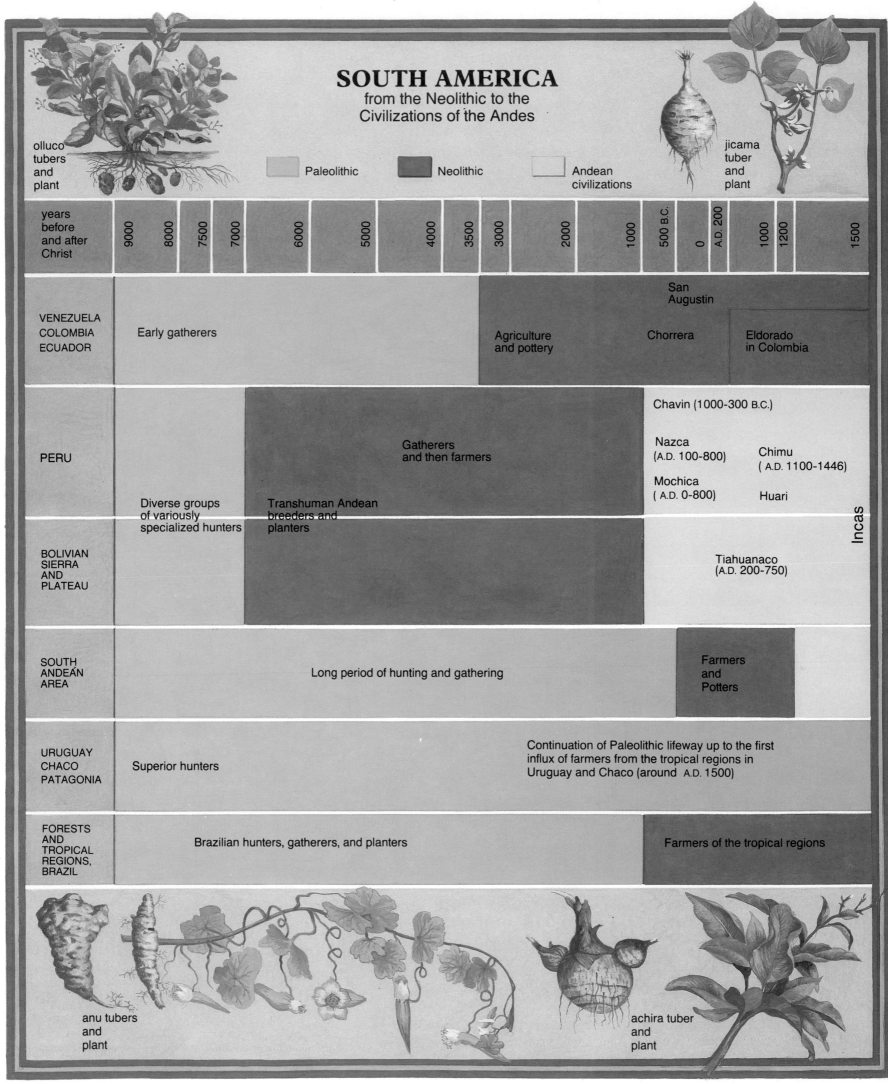

SOUTH AMERICA
from the Neolithic to the Civilizations of the Andes

olluco tubers and plant

jicama tuber and plant

| | Paleolithic | | Neolithic | | Andean civilizations |

years before and after Christ	9000	8000	7500	7000	6000	5000	4000	3500	3000	2000	1000	500 B.C.	0	A.D. 200	1000	1200	1500
VENEZUELA COLOMBIA ECUADOR	Early gatherers								Agriculture and pottery			San Augustin / Chorrera			Eldorado in Colombia		
PERU	Diverse groups of variously specialized hunters				Gatherers and then farmers							Chavin (1000-300 B.C.) / Nazca (A.D. 100-800) / Mochica (A.D. 0-800)			Chimu (A.D. 1100-1446) / Huari		Incas
BOLIVIAN SIERRA AND PLATEAU				Transhuman Andean breeders and planters										Tiahuanaco (A.D. 200-750)			
SOUTH ANDEAN AREA	Long period of hunting and gathering													Farmers and Potters			
URUGUAY CHACO PATAGONIA	Superior hunters								Continuation of Paleolithic lifeway up to the first influx of farmers from the tropical regions in Uruguay and Chaco (around A.D. 1500)								
FORESTS AND TROPICAL REGIONS, BRAZIL	Brazilian hunters, gatherers, and planters												Farmers of the tropical regions				

anu tubers and plant

achira tuber and plant

EARLY FARMERS AND POTTERS

In the Andes region, agriculture began with the cultivation of various plants in widely separated areas. Around 7000 B.C., people cultivated beans in northern Peru, and a variety of maize was grown in northwestern Argentina. Around 5900 B.C., maize appears in a rocky fault on the northern coast of Chile. Somewhat later, traces of poroto beans were found at Pichasca. These sporadic indicators show that some hunter-gatherer groups, in the Andean tradition, practiced a basic form of agriculture during a halt in their seasonal migration. At the same time, humans began to domesticate the llama. However, that process took about two thousand years.

local variety with a variety from southern Asia. The cultivation of cotton made possible the development of the important Peruvian craft of weaving.

In this new cultural phase, villages multiplied and grew. The art of decoration of baskets and gourd vessels also developed. Stone products of this phase were rather clumsy. The ax was the predominant tool.

During about 2000 B.C., religious ideas were reflected in complex funeral rites and in the construction of temples in both the coastal and mountainous regions. The architecture used squared stones held together with clay-based

among at least two groups that were active around 3200 B.C. This was at Puerto Hormiga, in the river region of northern Colombia, and at Valdivia, on the coast of Ecuador.

The Valdivia site is particularly interesting. After a phase characterized by local pottery, came a phase marked by splendid pottery with incised motifs, similar in numerous ways to the pottery of a contemporary Japanese culture known as Jomon. Thus, this was not simply a culture of modest fishermen, as was once thought. Valdivia had a large religious district, called Real Alto, with by far the oldest structure built on the platforms of the Peruvian Pre-

This container with its carved decorations was made from a large, hollowed-out gourd. (Huaca Prieta, Peru, 2000 B.C.)

This condor with a serpent on its breast is a decoration produced by applying a dye to cotton cloth. (Huaca Prieta, Peru, about 2000 B.C.)

These two ceramic statuettes were probably intended as fertility symbols. These are among the oldest-known pieces of South American pottery. (Valdivia, 3200-1800 B.C.)

From these starting points agriculture developed in the Andean and Peruvian regions. At the same time, new species of plants were used. Among these were the amaranth (a plant with seeds arranged in spikes), the cucurbitacae, the quinoa, and maize. Varieties of potatoes also originated. This entire process unfolded without the appearance of pottery, as is common almost everywhere in agriculture's early stages. Around 2500 B.C., another great innovation occurred. Cotton was produced by crossing a

mortar. In some instances, the sacred enclosures were erected on top of one or two platforms.

Origins and Spread of Pottery

The coastal areas of Colombia and Ecuador offer a different picture. There, clear traces of agriculture (including maize cultivation) can be traced back to 3000 B.C. Agriculture coexisted with a traditional diet based on seafoods. Pottery techniques originated in this region. Crockery with incised decorations was in common use

Ceramic. Real Alto had a large plaza surrounded by sacred mounds.

Through the centuries, pottery spread from this center. Archaeological data situates one primary region in Venezuela, in the western Amazon Basin, around 2000 B.C. Other important sites were in the Lake Titicaca region about 1200 B.C., and in northern Chile and northwestern Argentina around 500 B.C.

THE NORTHERN ANDEAN REGION

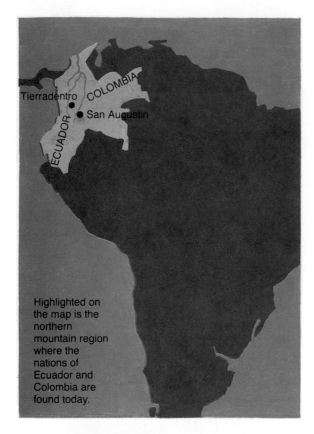

Highlighted on the map is the northern mountain region where the nations of Ecuador and Colombia are found today.

Characteristics of the Region

The mountainous areas of Colombia and Ecuador and the respective Pacific coasts represent a link in the climatic and topographical chain between the Central American area and the Andean area proper. The landscape offers a contrasting panorama—a hot and humid coastal region, a Cordillerian region with basins and temperate valleys, and the wild eastern slope. This variety of landscapes accounts for the diversity of regional cultures, the development of which was influenced by the cultures of Central America and the Andes.

Chorrera Pottery

In times of increasing circulation of products, early Neolithic communities multiplied. Religion developed into an important activity, and some villages were transformed into centers of worship. This tradition was continued by the Chorrera culture, the most important culture of Ecuador's "late development" period. This culture was known for the remarkable quality of its handmade painted pottery (1500-500 B.C.). Cultivation of maize underwent its greatest diffusion in the Guayas River basin.

The Monuments of San Augustin

The clearest expression of monument art in this area was that of San Augustin, a region near the source of the Magdalena River in southern Colombia. San Augustin has been dated at around 500 B.C.

Ritual and funerary centers were concentrated in a series of groups arranged in a circular pattern extending roughly 30 miles (50 km). The culture produced original monoliths that have only recently been discovered. These ancient stone structures were often found buried in the subsoil or beneath a tangle of vegetation. Their height varies from about 3 to 8 feet (1 to 2.5 m). Their roughness expresses a symbolism which is difficult to interpret. Among the various motifs is that of a man with feline features, sometimes wielding a weapon or symbolic instrument. Another interesting element is that of the "double" or "Second I," sometimes represented by an animal, sometimes in the form of a head with arms radiating outward over the person.

In the neighboring region of Tierradentro was a group with cultural ties to San Augustin. Its sculpture was much simpler. However, they constructed great tombs with walls and roofs painted in complicated geometrical patterns. This tradition has been preserved in a simplified manner in the semicircular burial chambers, which are entered through a vertical shaft. It is there that the body of the deceased was placed. It was surrounded by vases and other offerings.

On the left and on the opposite page: These two similar monoliths originally stood at the entrance to a megalithic temple. They represent a warrior with club in hand, his "Second I" hovering above his head. (San Augustin, Colombia) *Below:* Monolithic statues line the path leading to an underground temple in San Augustin.

Opposite page on top: This ceramic statuette is typical of Chorrera art, which reached its peak between the tenth and sixth centuries B.C.

The plan *(on the left)* and a cross section *(below)* show a temple hollowed out from the earth at Tierradentro. Entrance was gained through a vertical shaft with stairs. The ceiling was supported by two pillars.

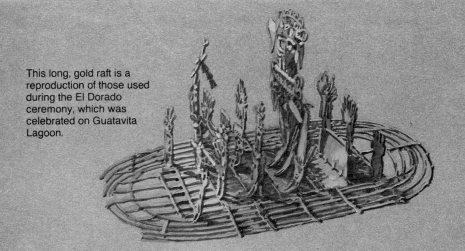

This long, gold raft is a reproduction of those used during the El Dorado ceremony, which was celebrated on Guatavita Lagoon.

Gold

At the beginning of the years A.D., various cultures developed in what is now Colombia. These groups lived in villages but rarely formed broader organizations. Following this was a period of regional development. Cultures in this period generally had an advanced technology. Also, they were sophisticated in the areas of arts and crafts. Their products included pottery that had great variation in both form and decoration, small statues, and small replicas of curved-roof dwellings that had large facades and single entrances. In some of these objects, one can see the influence of Central American art. This confirms that trade was carried on between Central and South America.

The highest development in the arts occurred among certain groups between about A.D. 500 and 1540. During this period, highly advanced techniques of working with gold were achieved.

These techniques included molding, soldering, hammering and alloying gold with copper, plus relief work and filigree. The art objects were usually found in large cemeteries. The objects included vessels of human and animal figures and various ornaments that were probably religious symbols.

Gold had no economic value for these people. However, because of its color and purity, it was considered to be a reflection of the sun, the highest deity worshiped by these people. One tale tells of a hero who was reincarnated as a tribal chief. Part of his investment ceremony involved sprinkling his body with powdered gold followed by a sailing ritual. This story, which gave rise to the legend of El Dorado, is recounted by one of the most important gold objects ever discovered —a small raft with crafted people on board.

A gold bottle in the shape of a squash (Quimbaya style) was found in Cauca Valley, Colombia.

A stylized man with a perforated pattern, was carved into a fragment of gold. (Tolima style).

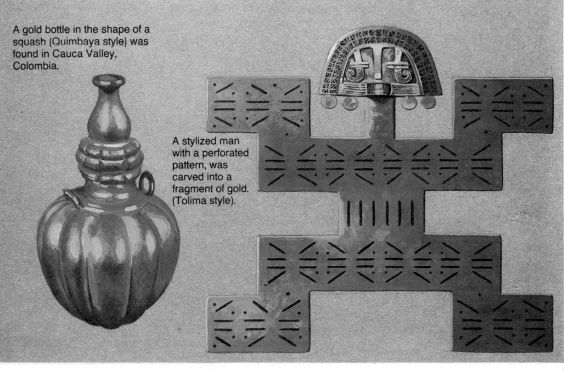

This view is of one of the terraces at Cerro Sechin (Chavin area). The carved pillars form a procession of priests and warriors. The oldest part of the temple foundations dates from before 1000 B.C.

In the inset: The lanzon, lance of Chavin (900 B.C.), is a monolith 13 feet (4 m) high embedded in the temple. It is decorated with a monstrous being in the form of a man and a cat. The lanzon was the center of Chavin society and the link between heaven and earth.

The Mochica culture is pictured in pink; the Chavin culture in yellow; and the Nazca culture in blue.

Remains of a Mochica temple were found in bricks of unfired earth, Chiquitoy, Peru.

ANDEAN CIVILIZATION

The Chavin Culture (1000-300 B.C.)

South American cultural development reached its highest levels in what is present-day Peru and northern Bolivia. In these areas, over just a few centuries, a number of cult centers came together to form an important nucleus whose center was located at a very prestigious temple complex called Chavin de Huantar. Its location was favorable to the blending of elements from the coast and the wilderness. The coast was characterized by rectangular architecture with platforms. The wilderness was characterized by decorations of jaguars, eagles, and serpents. The initial structure, which can be dated to 1000 B.C., had a series of interior galleries where initiation rites were probably practiced and where numerous offerings were placed.

At the intersection of two interior galleries, there exists, still intact, a column in the form of a spear.

The Chavin culture underwent a rapid expansion in the Sierra and along the coast. The Chavin centers suggest a stratified social order that was influenced by groups of priests. These areas were the rough basis for the first states and urban centers, with a high level of technical and artistic achievement. Archaeologists refer to this as the "classic" period or period of "regional flowering." The economy was based on a fully developed agriculture. Irrigation methods were practiced, and in mountainous regions, sides of hills were terraced for cultivation. Other major facets of the centers were the concentration of population, the intensity of commerce, and the working of gold. Social stratification was com-

Above: Some sculptors position stones in the desert, forming large figures, called geoglyphs. The Nazca desert thus witnessed the birth of some splendid artistic designs, completely visible only from a great height. In the background is a drawing of a monkey—one of the geoglyph patterns. In the inset is the outline of other gigantic figures: birds, reptiles, spiders, and a killer whale.

The head of a warrior-priest, painted in bright colors, is an example of Nazca pottery from the late fifth century A.D.

This polychrome pottery takes the form of a kneeling warrior. The great skill needed to capture the human face and its expressions is one of the characteristics of Mochica art.

Terra-cotta statues depicting two fishermen in light reed canoes are examples of Mochica art (Totora).

plex. Everything indicates that the government of priests had been replaced by a government of nobles and a monarchy, with the advent of a warrior class.

The Nazca Culture (A.D. 100-800)

The Nazca culture of Peru began to develop on the south coast around A.D. 100. There people produced decorated pottery. Decorations ranged from realistic depictions of plants and animals to abstract, complicated symbolism.

Nazca religious activities usually took place in the open. Markings found on rocks seem to be references to stars and the heavens. The Nazcas made furrows in the rocky soil. Some of these furrows were linear and may have been ritual pathways; other furrows were outlines of animals.

The Mochica Culture (A.D. 1-800)

The Mochica culture was centered in northern Peru. They developed an original architecture that utilized adobe bricks. The bricks were used for both dwellings and step-pyramids. The best examples are the Tombs of the Sun and the Moon, that face each other at the entrance to Moche Valley. The Mochica navigated along the coasts on boats made from reeds. They engaged in commerce and occasionally warred against neighboring groups. It is through their pottery that the activities of this group are known. Because of their tendency toward realism, they have been termed the "Greeks of America."

THE INCA EMPIRE

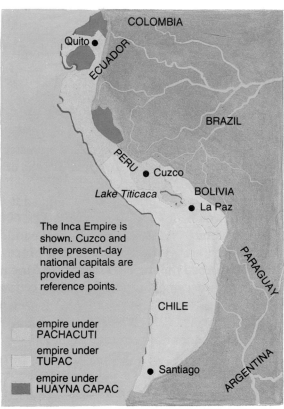

The Inca Empire is shown. Cuzco and three present-day national capitals are provided as reference points.

empire under PACHACUTI
empire under TUPAC
empire under HUAYNA CAPAC

The origins of the Inca Empire are surrounded in legend. It began as a small kingdom that, like neighboring kingdoms, had broken off from the empire of Huari. In A.D. 1438, the Inca Yupanki rose to power. He was a great warrior and statesman who had the title of Pachacuti, or "he who opens a new era." Under his rule, the Incas expanded outward from the capital city of Cuzco. This city became one of the greatest cities of early America.

The Three Conquerors

Inca traditions mention three sovereigns as the conquerors and organizers of the empire. In addition to being the first ruler, Pachacuti Inca Yupanki is also known for his reorganization of the empire on both political and social levels. His conquests included the areas of Peru closest to Cuzco and the Colla kingdom on Lake Titicaca. He was succeeded by his son, Tupac Inca Yupanki, who extended the empire to the central and southern coast of Peru, the southern Bolivian plateau, northwestern Argentina, and northern and central Chile. Huayna Capac, son of Tupac Inca Yupanki, enlarged and consolidated present-day Ecuador. There he established a second capital called Quito.

The End of the Empire

The eldest son and successor to Huayna Capac, Huascar, did not succeed in holding the empire together. Civil war broke out in the

On the left is a chart of Machu Picchu. Some of its features include: **1)** access stairway, **2)** terraced esplanades, center-city, **3)** solar observatory, **4)** steep sloped terrace-works, and **5)** temple of the "Three Windows."

Below: Machu Picchu is seen as it appears today. The alignment of the drawing and the chart are roughly the same. It is thus possible to locate the various parts of the city indicated on the chart, except for the access staircase.

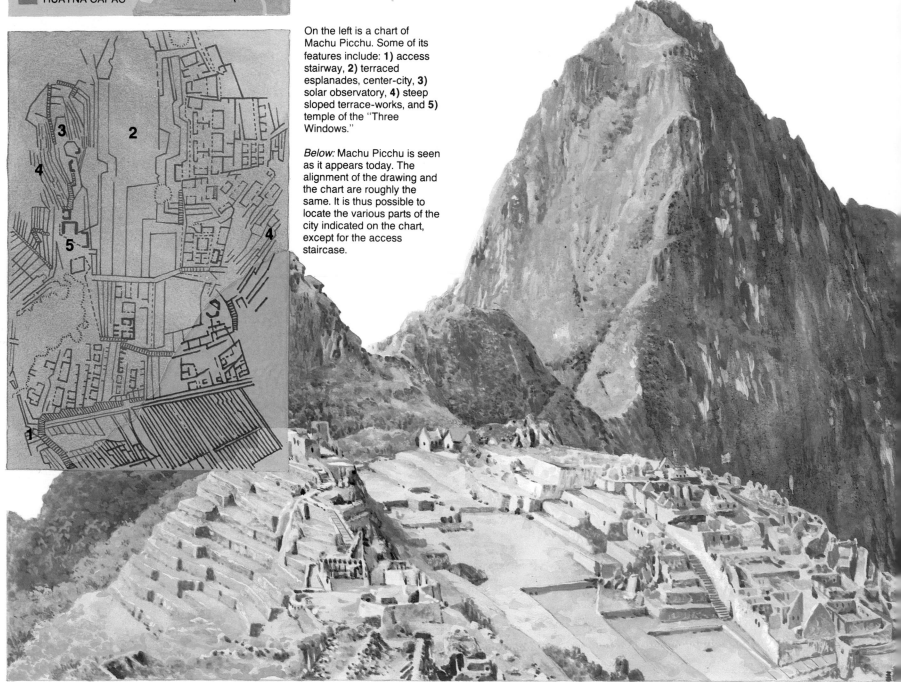

empire when Huascar's cousin, Atahuallpa, rose up against him and eventually defeated him in a bloody encounter.

A handful of Spaniards, led by Francisco Pizarro, were clever enough to take advantage of the confusion caused by the war. They imprisoned Atahuallpa in 1532 and condemned him to death the following year. The advent of a new ruler and the founding of the Spanish city of Lima, on the central coast, marked the fall of the Inca Empire. Their traditions, however, persisted among many of the Indian groups of the region.

Inca Culture

The Incas had three thousand years of Andean technological and cultural development. Their originality consisted above all in the organization of the empire, one of the greatest in history. The Inca sovereign was at the center of this system.

The widespread system of roads going out from Cuzco and extending in all directions was dotted with cities, villages, and stations. These roads were used by men transporting goods on llamas, by armed troops, and by the famous messengers known as chasqui. On the high southern hills, sacrificial rites were often celebrated in honor of the gods of sky and fertility.

The Incas were masters of monumental architecture, using perfectly fitted, massive stone blocks. The fortress of Sacsayhuaman near Cuzco and the high mountain cities of Machu Picchu and Ollantaytambo are the best examples. The basic framework was completed by terraces and gradually descending planes used for farming, irrigation canals, bridges, mines, and metalworking centers.

This statue depicts a man carrying an aribalo, a large vase characteristic of the Incas. These vases were often used to carry liquids. (Pachamac, fifteenth century A.D.)

On top: Scenes of Incan life, taken from documents left by the early Spaniards, are depicted: **1)** sowing of maize, **2)** hoeing and weeding of maize, **3)** harvesting of maize, **4)** a woman weaving on a simple loom, **5)** a messenger, or chasqui, who traveled on foot, delivering messages by word of mouth.

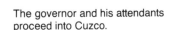
The governor and his attendants proceed into Cuzco.

This map shows population patterns and cultural influences between 2000 B.C. and the Christian Era.

This map shows the population patterns and cultural influences between the beginning of the Christian Era and A.D. 500.

Th
cultu
region
ern C
and t
broad
of the
cultu
tics, a
of po
Peru.
riving
B.C. in
and n
not oc

The
Per

Gro
in the
village
region
of eas
the Ch
ces be
menta
styles.
and se

In t
village
in loos
dwelli

Along a riverbend in the Amazon forest, a group of Indians, having arrived by canoe, has begun to build a village. The cabins are made of wood and, in the area where trees have been felled and the underbrush burned away, the people are planting manioc, using digging sticks. To the right, two boys are rotating a stick on top of a dry branch in order to start a fire. In the foreground, two women grate manioc tubers to make flour. Behind them, other women are weaving reed baskets. On the river, fish are being caught with a harpoon.

PEOPLE OF THE CARIBBEAN, THE AMAZON BASIN, AND EASTERN AND SOUTHERN BRAZIL

Between the eastern slopes of the Andes and the Atlantic Ocean lies a vast area of the continent that lacks the cultural level attained in the regions already examined. In some cases, there are groups acquainted with agriculture and pottery. In other cases, there is still the persistence of groups of hunters and gatherers, such as in the forests of the southeastern Brazil.

The Caribbean Basin

The Caribbean Basin covers the northern region of Venezuela and the islands of the Caribbean. Direct influences from the northern Andean region were felt here. One example was the barrancoid culture in the area around the Orinoco Delta. The pottery, which was painted with complex decorative patterns, flourished in the period between 1000 to 500 B.C. It resembled pottery which had developed in northern Colombia.

Other local traditions developed, whose existence was based on cultivation and in part on fishing and the gathering of seafood. Some groups were skilled in sailing and settled over a large part of the Antilles. Their descendants were the Caribs, the first Native Americans to come in contact with the Spanish.

Equatorial Forest and Tropical Savanna Regions

The Amazon River has the largest river basin in the world. The thick forest covering it was largely avoided by hunters. Once the Neolithic

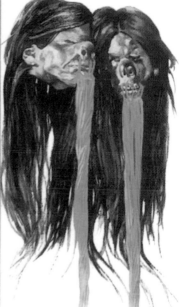

Directly above: Shown are the famous *Tsanta,* or skull-trophies, shrunken in size through a special process developed by the Jivaro Indians in the Amazon region of Ecuador. *On top:* This curved stone ax comes from the Paraná River and dates from about 5000 B.C.

This map reflects population movements and cultural influences between A.D. 1000 and 1520.

mode of life became established in the western mountain regions, scattered groups broke off and migrated. These groups took advantage of river currents, and eventually settled down at favorable sites along the river's banks. Recent archaeological excavations suggest the very early existence (4000 B.C.) of groups already familiar with pottery. Next came the Ananatuba group (1000 B.C.) that dwelt on the island of Marajo near the mouth of the Amazon.

Like the Ananatubas, other groups of farmers spread outward along the Amazon River basin and along Brazil's northern coast. Because the terrain was bare of rock except for occasional outcrops, their tools and other common objects were made of perishable materials. Research indicates that these people lived in isolated villages and, in addition to cultivating tropical plants (yucca, manioc, maize), lived by fishing,

hunting, and gathering.

The major change found by archaeologists was a polychrome, or multicolored, pottery in the area of the low Amazon River basin around A.D. 1000. This pottery included painted and incised funerary urns with geometrical symbols. There was also evidence of an increase in the number of villages along the waterways. The dead came to be buried in large mounds of earth, at times more than 165 feet (50 m) in diameter. There is also evidence of the beginning of social stratification. Certain Amazon tribes engaged in skull worship and headhunting. The most notable case was that of shrunken heads, typical of the Jivaro Indians of eastern Ecuador.

The Tupi-Guarani Expansion

A group of Amazon origin, the Tupi-Gua-

rani, expanded to the south, beginning in A.D. 500. This group was centered mainly in eastern Bolivia and Paraguay on one side, and along the entire Brazilian coast on the other.

The Guarani, whose cultural and linguistic mark is still evident on present-day populations, were known for a varied pottery. This included decorated funerary urns sometimes painted and sometimes typically ridged, with raised areas created by pressing with the fingers. Trade, as well as migrations of these groups, caused this pottery to be found from the central Amazon to the Parana Delta. A widely used tool was the polished stone ax, affixed to a long wooden handle. The villages consisted of common houses. These long houses were surrounded by a circular fence that provided defense during frequent attacks.

65

SOUTHERN CHILE, PATAGONIA, AND TIERRA DEL FUEGO

The Araucanians

The Maule River, located at the extreme southern border of the Incan presence, can also be considered as the southern border of the Andean cultural area. The territory farther to the south was, and in part still is, the land of the Mapuche, or Araucanian, people. These people developed from ancient populations of hunters, seafood gatherers, and groups of farmer-potters who arrived from central Chile between the fifth and tenth centuries A.D. They adapted to a humid climate and a wooded environment, partially conserving their hunting and gathering activities.

south of the Limay and Negro rivers, are descendants of hunters from the close of the Ice Age. These people specialized in hunting guanaco. Sometime during their development, they added the use of bow and arrows to that of the spear and bolas. Around A.D. 1700, some groups began to use pottery to a limited extent. The environmental and climatic limitations of the region, however, prevented agriculture from coming into practice. This is because agriculture could not be carried out without a complex irrigation system. Housing among the Tehuelche and the Ona of Tierra del Fuego consisted of leather tents. These tents were supported by

the northern coast of the Strait of Magellan. In ancient times, other groups had crossed that same stretch around 8000 B.C., immediately after the retreat of the glaciers. There is important evidence of their religious ceremonies, during which the men, completely naked in spite of the hostile climate, painted their bodies and covered their faces with large conical masks in order to give the gods material form.

The Canoeros

The wide, fanlike spread of islands which extends into the Pacific Ocean opposite the southern coast of Chile was populated by very

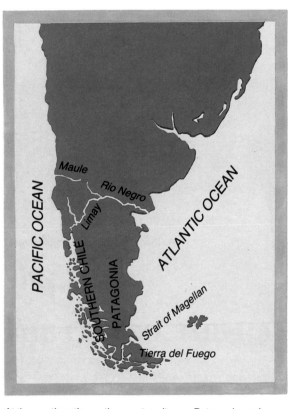

At the continent's southern extremity are Patagonia and Tierra del Fuego.

Two Araucanian women are seen in front of a ruca, which is a house with a straw roof.

The Pehuenche

The Pehuenche were a people adapted to the mountainous Argentina environment south of Mendoza and in the province of Neuquen. Sixteenth century chroniclers describe the traditions of these gatherers and migratory shepherds. In addition to intensive activity in the areas of hunting and vegetable gathering, these people are also known for their use of rock salt and their huge cliff carvings in the rocky regions north of Neuquen and in the surrounding Chilean valleys.

The Tehuelche

The Tehuelche, who settled in Patagonia

log posts from the Cordillera. Social organization coincided with the family structure. Because hunting was important, these people migrated with their prey to an extent. In the mesetas, it is still possible to find the tent supports and semicircular parapets built from stone that were used as stakeouts during hunting expeditions.

The Ona

The Ona were inhabitants of the northern plains of Tierra del Fuego. These people did not use horses and thus preserved their original way of life for a long time. At some indefinite date, their predecessors arrived across the sea from

specific types of natives. These people were extremely well adapted to the maritime environment. They lived mostly in cabins built on the coast and on the edges of the forested interior. Their main occupations were the gathering of mollusks along the shore and the harpoon-hunting of seals from canoes.

Groups of Canoeros were already present around 4000 B.C., and they continued their life of fishing for a thousand years. Around 2000 B.C., they added the activities of land hunting, mainly using bone harpoons. These inhabitants of the far edge of the world disappeared after the arrival of the Europeans. Many fell victim to diseases brought by the Europeans.

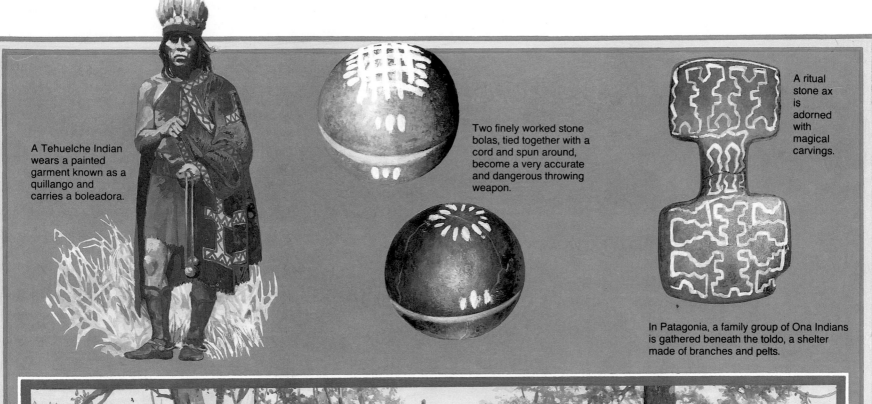

A Tehuelche Indian wears a painted garment known as a quillango and carries a boleadora.

Two finely worked stone bolas, tied together with a cord and spun around, become a very accurate and dangerous throwing weapon.

A ritual stone ax is adorned with magical carvings.

In Patagonia, a family group of Ona Indians is gathered beneath the toldo, a shelter made of branches and pelts.

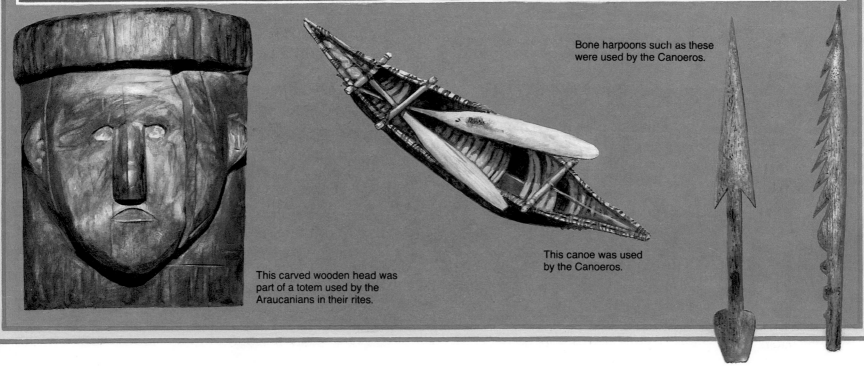

This carved wooden head was part of a totem used by the Araucanians in their rites.

This canoe was used by the Canoeros.

Bone harpoons such as these were used by the Canoeros.

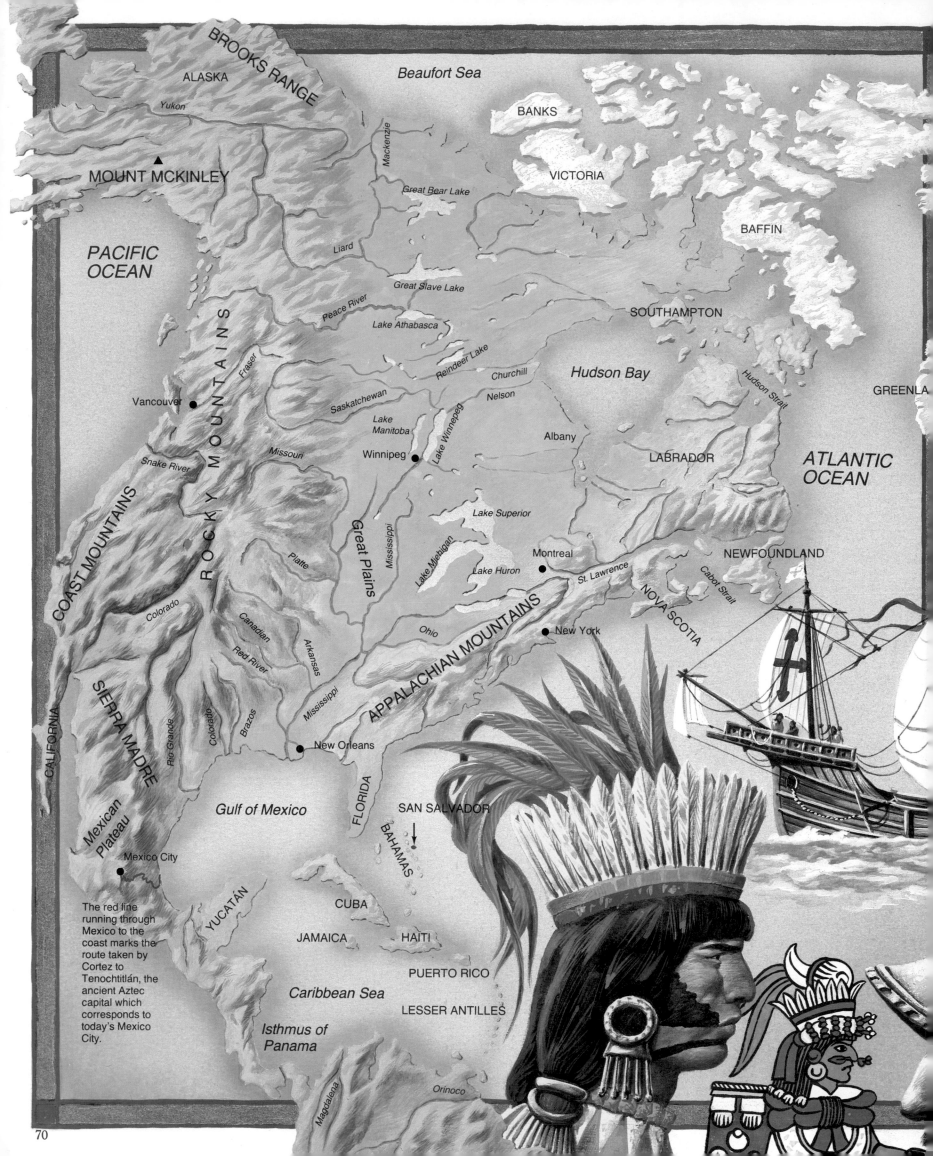

BROOKS RANGE

ALASKA

Beaufort Sea

Yukon

BANKS

VICTORIA

▲ MOUNT MCKINLEY

BAFFIN

PACIFIC OCEAN

Mackenzie

Great Bear Lake

Liard

Great Slave Lake

Peace River

SOUTHAMPTON

Lake Athabasca

Fraser

Reindeer Lake

Churchill

Hudson Bay

Hudson Strait

GREENLA

Vancouver •

Saskatchewan

Nelson

Snake River

Missouri

Lake Manitoba

Lake Winnipeg

Winnipeg •

Albany

LABRADOR

ATLANTIC OCEAN

Platte

Lake Superior

Great Plains

Mississippi

Lake Michigan

Lake Huron

Montreal •

St. Lawrence

NEWFOUNDLAND

Cabot Strait

Colorado

Canadian

Red River

Arkansas

Ohio

New York •

NOVA SCOTIA

Rio Grande

Colorado

Brazos

Mississippi

APPALACHIAN MOUNTAINS

New Orleans •

SIERRA MADRE

COAST MOUNTAINS

ROCKY MOUNTAINS

CALIFORNIA

Mexican Plateau

FLORIDA

Gulf of Mexico

SAN SALVADOR

↓

BAHAMAS

Mexico City •

The red line running through Mexico to the coast marks the route taken by Cortez to Tenochtitlán, the ancient Aztec capital which corresponds to today's Mexico City.

YUCATÁN

CUBA

JAMAICA

HAITI

PUERTO RICO

Caribbean Sea

LESSER ANTILLES

Isthmus of Panama

Magdalena

Orinoco

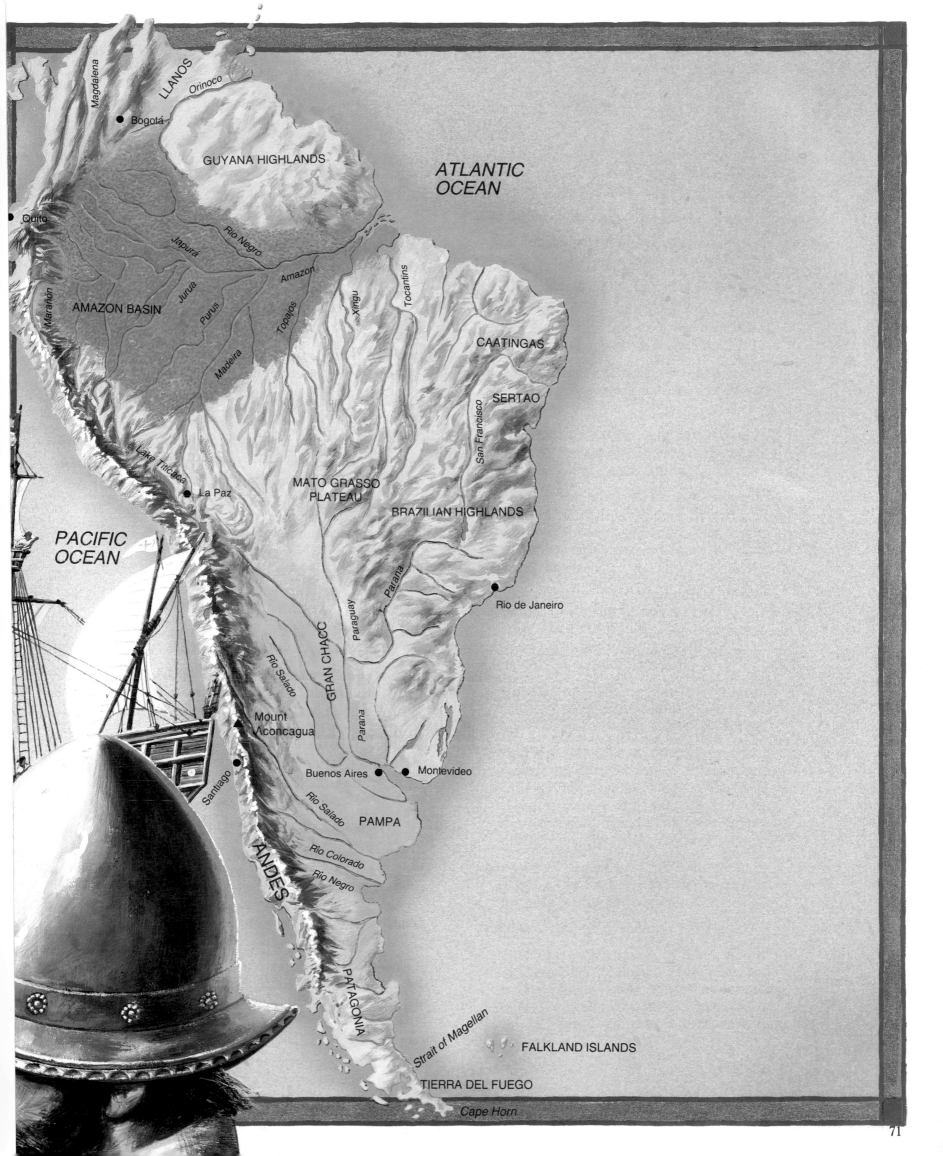

Magdalena

LLANOS

Orinoco

● Bogotá

GUYANA HIGHLANDS

ATLANTIC
OCEAN

● Quito

Japurá

Rio Negro

Marañón

Jurua

Purus

Amazon

AMAZON BASIN

Madeira

Topajos

Xingu

Tocantins

CAATINGAS

SERTAO

San Francisco

Lake Titicaca

● La Paz

MATO GRASSO
PLATEAU

BRAZILIAN HIGHLANDS

PACIFIC
OCEAN

Parana

Paraguay

GRAN CHACO

Rio Salado

Parana

● Rio de Janeiro

Mount
Aconcagua

Parana

ANDES

Santiago ●

Buenos Aires ●

● Montevideo

Rio Salado

PAMPA

Rio Colorado

Rio Negro

PATAGONIA

Strait of Magellan

FALKLAND ISLANDS

TIERRA DEL FUEGO

Cape Horn

71

fauna: the animals that live and thrive in a specific environment at a specific period in time. The fauna of any place on earth is determined by the ability to adapt to and thrive in the existing environmental conditions.

fertile: rich in natural resources; able to produce and/or reproduce.

flora: the plants that grow in a specific environment at a specific period of time. The earth's flora varies from place to place.

fossil: a remnant or trace of an organism of a past geologic age, such as a skeleton or leaf imprint, embedded in some part of the earth's crust. Scientists search for fossils as a way of learning about past life.

glaciers: gigantic moving sheets of ice that covered great areas of the earth in an earlier time. Glaciers existed primarily in the Pleistocene period, one million years ago.

Haab: the solar and civil calendar of the Maya Indians that includes 365 days.

harpoon: a spearlike weapon with a barbed head used in hunting whales and large fish.

herbivore: an animal that eats plants. Elephants and deer are herbivores.

hieroglyphic: a type of writing used mainly by ancient Egyptians in which certain signs and symbols (instead of letters) were used to represent words.

humid: containing a large amount of water or water vapor; damp. Warm air currents floating through coastal areas produce a humid climate.

hydraulic: operated by the movement and force of liquid; operated by the pressure created where a liquid is forced through a tube.

hypothesis: a theory based on available supporting evidence.

immigrate: to move into a new region or country.

implement: a tool or utensil used to perform some specific activity.

irrigate: to carry or deliver water to dry land by artificial means such as tunnels or ditches.

kivas: ritual structures of the Pueblo Indians, resembling old style pithouses.

lava: melted rock that flows from an erupting volcano.

lunar: having to do with the moon and its changing phases.

mammoth: a type of large, hairy elephant with curved tusks that is now extinct.

migrate: to move from place to place in search of food and shelter. Migration usually revolves around seasonal changes.

mollusk: any of a large group of animals having soft bodies enclosed in hard shells. Snails, oysters, and clams are mollusks.

monarch: the primary ruler of a state or kingdom, such as a king or queen.

monolith: something carved or formed from a single stone block.

mural: a large picture or scene painted on or attached to a wall.

nomad: a member of a tribe or people having no permanent home, but roaming about constantly in search of food and shelter.

oasis: special areas in a desert that have small reservoirs of water that allow the growth of trees and other plants.

obsidian: black, glasslike rock used in making small tools and ornaments.

pelt: the skin of an animal.

perishable: likely to spoil.

petroglyphs: stone carvings created by the interior peoples of early North America.

pirogue: a type of boat or canoe made by hollowing a log.

pithouse: a house formed by digging a deep hole in the ground and then covering the top with mats or bark.

plateau: an elevated and more or less level expanse of land.

plumage: the feathers of a bird.

portico: a porch or covered walkway.

precipitation: water droplets that are condensed in the earth's atmosphere to form rain, sleet, or snow.

primitive: of or existing in the beginning or earliest times; ancient.

prosperous: having good fortune; successful.

ritual: a system of ceremonies or procedures, especially with regard to religious worship.

sanctuary: a place of peace or safety; a haven or place of rest; a special building set aside for holy worship.

sarcophagus: a large tomb, usually heavily decorated or inscribed.

shaman: a medicine man or other wise person of certain Indian tribes in the Americas; a magician.

solar: of or having to do with the sun or the sun's energy.

species: a specific type or class of plant or animal.

subjugate: to conquer and force into servitude or slavery.

temperate: a climate that is neither very cold nor very hot, but rather moderate.

terrace: a raised flat mound of earth with sloping sides.

theocracy: a type of government in which the church has priority over and rules the state.

tributary: a small river or stream that usually flows into and is eventually part of a larger one.

tuber: a plant whose fruit develops and grows under the ground.

tundra: the immense, frozen plains of the Arctic and Antarctic.

Tzolkin: the religious calendar of the Maya Indians that included 260 days.

urn: a large vase or receptacle.

valley: a space of low land wedged between hills or mountains that usually has a stream flowing through it.

vessel: a bowl, pot, or other receptacle used for holding or containing something.

E

earthworks, 18-19, 22
ecosystems, 26
El Dorado, 55
Eric the Red, 5
Eriksson, Leif, 5
Eskimos, 5, 24-25

F

farming, 12-13, 22, 49, 52-53
fishing, 10, 51
fire, use of, 28
fjords, 10
Four Corners region, 12

G

gathering, 8-9, 17, 28, 51, 52
geoglyphs, 57
glaciation, 6, 27, 50
Grave Creek Mound, 20
grave goods, 20, 43
Great Basin, 8
Great Serpent Mound, Ohio, 20-21
"Greeks of America," 57

H

Haab, 45
head-hunting, 65
hieroglyphics, 41, 42
Hohokam, 12-13
Homo sapiens, 5, 6, 50
Hopewell culture, 20
Huari, 59
Huascar, 60
Huayana Capac, 60
Huehueteotl, 33, 37
Huitzilopochtli, 37
hunting, 6, 11, 16-17, 20, 24-25, 28, 50-51, 52
  bison, 16-17
  caribou, 24, 26-27
  guanaco, 68
  seal, 24-25

I

Ice Age, 6, 50
igloo, 25
Incas, 60-61
Indian, 5
Indian Knoll, Kentucky, 19
Inuit, 24-25
Ipiutak culture, 24-25

irrigation methods, 56
Itzá, 47

J, K

jaguar (as symbol), 31, 40-41
Japanese Current, 10
Jivaro Indians, 65
Jomon period, 53
kalasasaya, 59
kiva, 14

L

La Aguada culture, 62
language, 5, 12
Late period, 62
Late Prehistoric period, 22
lodge, 17

M

Major Temple, 37
Matacos, 66
Maya, 44-45, 48
Mayan cities, styles of, 46
Meadowcroft Shelter, 7, 20
Mesa Verde, 14
Mesoamerica, 28-49
  early inhabitants, 28
metalworking, 20, 43, 62
metals, 20, 55
Mexica, 37
Middle period
  (Andes regions of South America), 62
migration, human, 6-7, 9, 26, 48, 50
Mimbres (Mogollon subgroup), 13
Mississippian people, 22
Mixcoatl, 36
Mixtecs, 43
Mochica culture, 57
Mogollon, 12-13
monolith, 54
Monte Albán, 42
Monticula J, 42
mosaics, 43
mound building, 20
mountains, 4

N

Nauhyotzin, 37
Nazca culture, 57
nomadic people, 28, 37
Norsemen (see Viking)
North America, 6-27